OLDEST ALLIES

Alcantara 1809

RENÉ CHARTRAND

First published in Great Britain in 2012 by Osprey Publishing,
Midland House, West Way, Botley, Oxford, OX2 0PH, UK
44-02 23rd Street, Suite 219, Long Island City, NY 11101, USA

E-mail: info@ospreypublishing.com

A CIP catalogue record for this book is available from the British Library

Print ISBN: 978 1 84908 588 5
PDF ebook ISBN: 978 1 84908 589 2
ePub ebook ISBN: 978 1 78096 895 7

Page layout by bounford.com
Index by Rob Munro
Typeset in Sabon
Maps by bounford.com
3D BEV by Alan Gilliland
Originated by PDQ Media, Bungay, UK
Printed in China through Worldprint Ltd.

12 13 14 15 16   10 9 8 7 6 5 4 3 2 1

Osprey Publishing is supporting the Woodland Trust, the UK's leading
woodland conservation charity, by funding the dedication of trees. To
celebrate the Queen's Diamond Jubilee we are proud to support the
Woodland Trust's Jubilee Woods Project.

www.ospreypublishing.com

Artist's note

Readers may care to note that the original paintings from which the
colour plates in this book were prepared are available for private sale.
All reproduction copyright whatsoever is retained by the Publishers.
All inquiries should be addressed to:

mark@mrstacey.plus.com

The Publishers regret that they can enter into no correspondence upon
this matter.

CONTENTS

INTRODUCTION

Between January 1809, when Gen Sir John Moore's British army evacuated northern Spain at Corunna, and May, when Maj-Gen Sir Arthur Wellesley's campaigns liberated northern Portugal, British and French forces fought many engagements, raids and counter-raids in the area around Alcantara, Spain, and as far north as Ciudad Rodrigo and Salamanca. Outside of Wellesley's recapture of Porto from the French Marshal Soult, this period remains somewhat shrouded into an historical haze. Although no major battles involving tens of thousands of men occurred that drew sustained attention from historians, many engagements of vital strategic and tactical importance occurred, involving only a few hundred or a few thousand men. These actions in western Spain, which succeeded in mobilizing a major part of a French army corps, are the 'missing link' in the chronology of the Peninsular War, and are the subject of our study.

This period of the war, featuring little-known (and often unrecorded) raids and engagements, can be grouped together under one name – Alcantara – for it was here that the largest of these engagements was fought. But because of its strategic situation Alcantara was more than just a place to raid; it was the crossroads of one of the main mountain passes that could become an invasion route by either side. Hence, the engagement at Alcantara on 14 May 1809, which is mainly remembered because it occurred in a most scenic setting complete with a magnificent Roman bridge, was merely the final chapter in a period of raids that had been going on since January 1809. In those months, dozens and perhaps hundreds of raids and minor skirmishes took place; first in the plains of Leon until the action moved south to the isolated countryside of Estremadura.

For the sake of this study, we have tried to keep the narrative down to two main areas of action: northern Portugal and western Spain. There were also epic struggles going on in, for instance, the heroic city of Zaragoza and in eastern Spain. However, although it does not seem evident at first glance, the actions that went on in northern Portugal and western Spain were linked; indeed it could be argued that they were linked closely. They were elements

CIRCA AD 105

Bridge at Alcantara built

of one of the numerous plans and counter-plans that emerged at this time. For the French, it was Napoleon's master plan for subduing Portugal from several directions at once, and its effects, which is discussed in the main and lengthy first three chapters on origins, strategy and planning. It was also where guerrilla warfare was emerging.

As outlined in these pages, the arrival of the largely British-trained and led Loyal Lusitanian Legion that was deployed in raid warfare was crucial; with Spanish and Portuguese levies, it managed to perform not just one, but a myriad of raids big and small while deployed on the plains of Leon and this, in effect, isolated three French army corps (Marshal Victor's 1st, Soult's 2nd and Ney's 6th) by driving a wedge between northern and southern Spain along its mountainous border with Portugal. The important link between the French armies was essentially severed for months; coordination between the French marshals was next to impossible due to cut-off communications, and this was prevalent right up to the final epic battle at Alcantara.

The famous Roman bridge at Alcantara. It was built at the beginning of the 2nd century AD at the behest of Emperor Trajan. It is still in use today. (Author's photo)

ORIGINS

Alcantara

Alcantara is a small frontier town in the Spanish province of Estremadura, lying on the banks of the river Tagus near the border with Portugal. The town was originally founded by the Moors, on account of the convenience of a fine Roman stone bridge. As recorded in an AD 105 inscription over one of its arches, it was built during the reign of the Emperor Trajan (r.98 to 117) at the expense of the people of the Roman province of Lusitania. A Roman army camp is said to have been nearby, probably at the site of the present town. This excellent bridge was undoubtedly a major factor in encouraging trade and commerce in the domains of Hispania and Lusitania, as Spain and Portugal were initially called. The western Roman Empire eventually collapsed in the 5th century at the hands of the barbarian Visigoths, but the sturdy bridge over the Tagus remained. In the 8th century, the Muslim Moors invaded and settled in most of Christian Spain and Portugal. A small town was founded near the bridge, and it became known to the Moors as al-Quantara, which translates simply as 'the bridge'. Soon, the Christians set about winning back the domains lost to the Moors. and for centuries waged a more or less ceaseless war against them that is remembered as the *Reconquista* – the reconquest.

The town of Alcantara was first taken by the Christian army of King Ferdinand II of Leon in 1167, but it was retaken by the Moors five years later. In 1214, the army of King Alfonso IX of Leon captured Alcantara and the custody of the town was first granted to the knights of the Order of Calatrava; however, two years later, the knights of the Order of St Julian del Parero became the keepers of the town. Instituted in 1156, this knightly order soon changed its name to the Order of Alcantara, at the same time assuming a green colour for the cross whose tips ended in lilies, which they wore on their long white cloaks. As with all Christian knightly orders of the time, the Order of Alcantara also bore a religious character. In the following decades and centuries, the knights of Alcantara became a wealthy order thanks to battle successes against the Moors as well as substantial donations from pious Christians. In 1492, the *Reconquista* came to an end with the fall of Moorish Grenada to the Spanish Christian armies.

Walls had been built around the town in Moorish times and were maintained by the knights during the Middle Ages. They decayed thereafter, but remains can still be seen. During this period Alcantara still had a military role with regard to Portugal which, following the end of the campaigns against the Moors, had become a fiercely independent rival. After the two nations were united by a dynastic arrangement in 1580, the knights assumed a less warlike and more peaceful role, but nevertheless continued to prosper. By the late 16th century, the Order of Alcantara had some 37 'commanderies' of knights and was responsible in one way or another for about 53 castles or small towns in western Spain. It was, at that time, one of the more important knightly orders in the country.

Since the 15th century, the town had become the home of several religious orders besides the knights. The convents of St Francis and of the nuns of San Remedio were built. In 1495, the Knights of Alcantara settled on building their own convent as the seat of their order. This was approved by King Ferdinand and Queen Isabella. Construction of the knights' beautiful convent of San Benito de Alcantara began in 1499 and went on for most of the 16th century. Its cloister was built in the Gothic style on the foundations of a Moorish fort, but its most gracious feature was (and is) its three-storey Renaissance arches.

The Portuguese were not content with their union under the Spanish crown and, from 1640, proclaimed the Duke of Braganza as King John IV of Portugal and staged a successful 'war of restoration' (although Spain only formally

The arch on the bridge with the coat of arms of Spain at the top with, below, the inscription left by the Romans in the reign of Emperor Trajan that dates its inauguration to 105 AD. This area was the scene of the heaviest fighting on 14 May 1809. The Loyal Lusitanian Legion was posted at the far end. (Author's photo)

SUMMER 1807

French troops begin to move into Spain

accepted Portugal's independence in 1668). While Estremadura often bore the brunt of the border raiding and was impoverished by the depredations caused by the armed forces of both sides, there were no major engagements and Alcantara itself remained basically unscathed during this war.

The War of the Spanish Succession (1702–1714) brought warfare to the area and, in 1706, Alcantara was taken and sacked by Portuguese troops who then retired to their own borders. The next century was a fairly peaceful period for the town and its knights, whose position, by then, was more as noble country gentlemen enjoying a quiet life rather than as ferocious warriors. By the late 18th century, Alcantara had a population of about 5,000 inhabitants. Clouds of political instability appeared with the French Revolution of 1789; before long, most of Europe was engaged in warfare that eventually saw the rise of Napoleon Bonaparte who became Emperor of the French in 1804.

In the 1790s, Spain had first fought the French republicans, then switched sides and allied itself with the French to fight Britain, the common enemy. The loss of most of the Spanish fleet at the disastrous 1805 battle of Trafalgar greatly humbled the Spanish and there were murmurs and resentments about the French alliance. On the other hand, the Emperor of the French had defeated every large power on the continent, so it was out of the question to break the alliance.

As time passed, Napoleon became increasingly displeased with the 'neutral' kingdom of Portugal. That country was well known as 'Britain's oldest ally' with strong ties between these two maritime nations that went back to the Middle Ages. The Spanish and the Portuguese had not evolved a great liking for each other over the centuries, but there was a tolerance of sorts. There had even been, under French pressure, the short and somewhat ridiculous 1801 'War of the Oranges' between the two nations, who clearly did not wish a bloody contest. By 1807, Napoleon had had enough of Spain's inaction regarding Portugal's obvious double-dealing with the British. He wanted his continental blockade to be effective and starve Britain. Yet here was this huge gap: Portugal's coast as well as colonies such as Portuguese Brazil, flaunting the blockade while proclaiming to its adherence.

A view of the monastery of San Benito, built from the late 15th century as the seat of the knightly Order of Alcantara. (Author's photo)

This had to stop. During the summer of 1807, large contingents of French troops moved into Spain and its allied Spanish army was advised to be alert at the Portuguese border.

Invasion of Portugal

The French plan to solve the problem was to invade Portugal. A Spanish army was tasked to occupy Porto and the north of the country while a French army would take Lisbon and hold the south. Both France and Spain agreed to partition Portugal and its colonies to their benefit. However, the sight of thousands of French troops marching southwest across their country filled many ordinary Spaniards with unease. Napoleon had marched his armies into every country in western Europe; now it was Portugal's turn, but some Spaniards wondered whether tomorrow it might be theirs. For now, the Spanish had to submit to France, which was the ally of their own government, but resentment and mistrust rose in their hearts.

Meanwhile, in Lisbon, everyone realized that the game was up and that the French were moving across Spain and being joined by a sizeable Spanish force. It was unlikely that the Portuguese army could resist such an invasion. Although sweeping reforms to the organization of the regular army and the reserves had been decreed since 19 May 1806, they had not been totally implemented. It was theoretically wonderful and the new uniforms looked good, but the old laissez-faire habits within the regular army did not vanish and the officer corps, while giving lip service to the reforms, was divided on the wisdom of such measures. The regular army was way below its establishment strength and could muster, at most, 25,000 men. Of these

General Junot's French infantry crossing the mountains along the upper Tagus River from Spain into Portugal, November 1807. The border areas between Spain and Portugal were rife with natural obstacles, such as mountain ranges, which made their crossing very difficult, especially for large armies. (Print after Maurice Orange. Private collection. Author's photo)

perhaps 10,000 to 15,000 might be fit to take the field. Its most influential senior officer, the Marquis de Alorna, was openly pro-French and felt Portugal's long-term salvation lay in becoming part of the pan-European empire mooted by Napoleon. General Gomes Freire de Andrade with some intellectuals felt there could be no other solution. Even the British felt that defending Portugal against Napoleon's troops – augmented by a Spanish contingent – was impossible. Creating a 'front' there was hopeless, and resisting France and Spain was lunacy.

This was the prevailing opinion in European capitals, and it was totally discouraging to any patriotic Portuguese. Fighting, or even resisting, seemed like suicide. Thus, in November, the large French army of 30,000 men – assembled at Alcantara under General Andoche Junot and, assisted by General Caraffa's 25,000 Spanish troops further north – easily marched into Portugal. Indeed, its main problem turned out to be crossing the mountains that line the border between Spain and Portugal, due to the difficult topography and Portugal's lack of good roads. With the Portuguese army still inefficient and its command deeply divided, the Spanish contingent cautiously entered the north and eventually reached and peacefully occupied Porto, a city of 30,000 inhabitants. The main thrust of the invasion was Junot's French army further south. Hoping to avoid a long siege at Elvas, Junot opted instead to follow the upper river Tagus, pass Alcantara, and cross into Portugal through the mountains. It was a daring gamble, but, as there were no forces to oppose him, it worked, and on 25 November Junot's army occupied Castelo Branco. From there, the French army could march four or five days and reach Lisbon; it brushed aside what little resistance it met and progressed steadily towards the capital.

At the royal palace in Lisbon, Prince Regent Joao VI knew that Junot would soon be at the gates. Some of his officials, officers and courtiers were preparing to rally to the French. Others were disheartened and lost hope for their nation's future, and they were right; Napoleon mooted plans for the partition of Portugal into several fiefdoms. Obviously, any fierce resistance would cause a fruitless bloodbath in the capital. At this desperate time, Joao VI made an extraordinary decision that saved both the crown and Portugal. Instead of bending his knee to the Emperor Napoleon and the invading army, he opted to leave Lisbon and go to Brazil, Portugal's immense territory in America, taking with him the royal family and all those at court who wished to follow him.

Many did not wish to endure a French occupation, especially as some officials might be sought by the French secret police. On 27 November, Joao VI, with some 15,000 people, embarked on a large fleet and sailed out of the river Tagus. As the Portuguese knew, Brazil was hardly a desperate place to spend exile, but instead a flourishing country with over four million souls, speckled with large cities, its own military forces and untold resources. Of course, there were no precedents in modern history for such a move by a royal family and its immediate effects were obvious. The legitimate Portuguese government still existed and was now waiting in exile for better days in which to fight Napoleon's imperial rule. No matter what the French did in occupied Portugal, its people's hearts and souls would always look towards its true rulers in Rio, whom no French minions could replace.

On 30 November, General Junot entered Lisbon with his troops, only to find that the palace was empty and that the Portuguese fleet had sailed to America. Junot and, eventually, Napoleon were most upset that Joao VI had 'escaped', and French propaganda immediately portrayed him as a lackey of the British, who had abandoned his people instead of embracing the wise and better values of a Napoleonic Europe. But popular wisdom throughout Europe was not convinced. By going to Brazil, the prince and the court had taken the only possible option other than becoming prisoners of the French emperor, even if he might keep them in a gilded cage.

French occupation

However, for the time being, the French ruled the country. The Portuguese people hoped that it would be a decent and mild regime, but sadly, they were soon disappointed. The sneering and somewhat despotic French generals governing the major cities and provinces treated the ordinary Portuguese almost as sub-humans. This outlook was often shared by their soldiers, who scorned the perceived backwardness of not only the Portuguese, but also their Spanish allies. This was a potentially lethal attitude because both the Portuguese and the Spanish people were (and remain) intensely proud. It could be said that, unlike their Spanish neighbours, the Portuguese were less likely to react with arrogance and bravado. More quiet, patient and orderly in their ways, they took the long view that, one day, things would change. And so they bided their time.

One of the first things General Junot did, by an order of 22 December 1807, was to disband the Portuguese army; this was followed by the disbanding of the militia and the Ordenanza in January and February 1808. The only Portuguese still free were those in exile in Brazil and the thousands who had fled elsewhere, notably England. As will be seen below, these latter were destined to play, with their British allies, an outstanding military role in the years ahead.

Meanwhile, increasing resentment was quietly filling the hearts and minds of the people of the Iberian Peninsula. Even in Spain, which was then an allied nation, the French troops conducted themselves deplorably, behaving as arrogant rogues toward all classes of society. As far as occupied Portugal was concerned things were even worse, for it seemed there were no bounds to what French soldiers would do. In Porto and the north, whose ancient wine trade with Britain was now ruined, resentment of the French occupation was great. The French, instead of soothing feelings by offering new opportunities, such as facilitating exports to markets elsewhere in continental Europe, went into a vicious cycle of repression. At Porto, squads of French soldiers would turn up at people's homes during the night or in broad daylight to take away suspects whose subsequent fate was likely to be torture and death. General of Division Jean-Baptiste-Maurice Loison was a good battlefield commander, but he forever tarnished his name by being associated with terrible deeds carried out on helpless people. The one-armed man who

presided over these cruel proceedings was nicknamed 'Maneta' by the Portuguese, and to this day, a popular, blackly humorous saying in Portugal is *Foi para o Maneta* ('Brought in to see Maneta'), uttered when things are really going badly for someone.

To complicate matters even further, the Catholic Church exerted immense influence and power in Iberia. Both Portugal's Braganza and Spain's Bourbon royal families were anointed by the Pope and a great many of their subjects believed that it was God's will that they sat on the thrones of their respective nations. There were as many sinners in Spain and Portugal as anywhere, but across all levels of society the people were unquestioning supporters of the Church – perhaps to a greater extent than anywhere else. This relative harmony between church and state in the Iberian kingdoms made the events and excesses of the French Revolution totally alien to any Spaniard and Portuguese. They were deeply disturbed by the French revolutionaries' actions such as the banning of the Catholic Church, the executions of the French royal family and countless priests, the seizure – often by the army –

General Junot, commander of the French invasion forces. (Anne S.K. Brown Military Collection, Brown University Library, Providence, USA)

of churches and monasteries, and the creation of a new calendar to replace the Christian one. General Bonaparte's rise to power and his toleration of the Catholic Church in France somewhat eased opinions, but his rise to Emperor, even if 'blessed' by the Pope, was seen with deep suspicion.

Now that Portugal had been occupied and its people were helpless against the exactions of the French troops, Napoleon actually sent more contingents over the Pyrenees; by early 1808, some 70,000 French troops were in the Iberian Peninsula. But now, they also acted with much disregard towards the Spanish. In some cases, churches were taken over and used as stables for French cavalry units, just as they had been in Portugal; to the devout Spaniards, such actions were a sacrilege. Relations between the 'allies' were rapidly deteriorating. There was also a darker side to the increase in French troop levels in Spain; Napoleon wanted to get rid of the 'degenerate' Bourbons on the Spanish throne, chase the knavish Prime Minister Manuel Godoy from power and make his brother Joseph king, to govern and 'modernize' Spain with the backing of the French army. There were already pro-French elements amongst the nobility and the intellectual classes who had been seduced by propaganda into thinking that a Napoleonic administration would end the old 'corrupt' ways and bring forth true progress. Sooner or later, reasoned Napoleon, the people would rally to his rule as they would benefit from such advantages as the legal 'Code Napoleon' and the benefits of a central administration.

Uprisings

Had there been some respect shown towards the population and an attempt to convince the peoples of Iberia that there were real benefits to being part of a greater Napoleonic Europe, it might have worked. Indeed, it had worked

2 MAY 1808

'Dos de Mayo' rebellion in Madrid

The 'Dos de Mayo' 1808 in Madrid. On 2 May 1808, thousands of Spaniards rose in Madrid against the French soldiers in the city – it was the start of the Peninsular War that soon enflamed all of Spain and Portugal. (Painting by Francisco Goya. Museo del Prado, Madrid. Author's photo)

The 'Tres de Mayo' 1808 in Madrid. A French firing squad going about its grim business inspired this powerful masterpiece of world art by Francisco Goya. The unexplainably gruesome and cruel French repressions in Spain and Portugal sparked a 'blood and death' reaction that resulted in some of the darkest episodes in modern warfare. Such scenes, alas, also occurred at Alcantara when Gen Lapisse's 2nd French Division captured the town. (Museo del Prado, Madrid. Author's photo)

to some extent in Germany and Poland. However, on 2 May 1808, the population of Madrid raised the standard of revolt against the French. The French repression was unsurprisingly quite ferocious, with hundreds of Spaniards slain in fighting or by French firing squads. Far from cowing the people, the reaction to the 'Dos de Mayo' (2 May) became the rallying cry for uprisings that started to break out elsewhere. Soon, all of Spain was in turmoil as the revolt became general.

The news of the uprisings in Madrid rapidly spread to Portugal and first reached Porto in early June. Occupied Portugal had been enduring abuse at the hands of the detested French army, but it was not only the Portuguese that revolted. Lt Gen Taranco's Spanish corps of some 6,000 troops was in Porto and, on 6 June, joined the Portuguese patriots and seized the city's French governor. The same day, Col Francisco de Silveira at Vila Real rallied the Portuguese patriots who proclaimed him general of the forces in the upper Douro valley. In the following days, the revolt spread to Braga, Melgaço and Braganza, where the aged Gen Manuel José Gomes de Sepulveda called on all veterans of units disbanded by the French to re-form their old units and for all patriots to join them. Many thousands did, and the Portuguese national flag flew again over Braganza's medieval castle, one of the kingdom's great symbols of its independence.

A major problem for the Portuguese patriots was their lack of leaders and good officers; many had gone to Brazil and others had joined the

French Portuguese Legion. At last, on 16 June, strong leadership emerged from a rather unusual source: the Church. Dom Pedro Pitoes, Bishop of Porto, took up the mantle and assumed supreme command, military as well as civil, of northern Portugal. Indeed, he felt he had authority over any liberated area in the country as president of the Junta (or council) organized to rule in the name of the royal family in Brazil. For now, this concerned mainly northern Portugal. The Bishop of Porto proved to be an energetic, shrewd, influential and resilient official who had great leadership qualities. He was especially good at rallying the people to the cause of the nation's independence, but his tactical military abilities were, understandably, very limited.

By mid-June 1808, the Portuguese uprising was general; the French occupation troops were everywhere on the defensive. The organization of the patriotic forces in the north of the country soon revolved around the Bishop of Porto. In July 1808, he contacted the Chevalier de Souza, Portugal's ambassador in London, for help from Great Britain. He wanted

Dom Pedro Pitoes, Bishop of Porto, c. 1808. This energetic cleric assumed command of the Portuguese government and its forces in northern Portugal. (Contemporary print. Museu Militar do Porto. Author's photo)

'three million Crusades' to buy supplies and pay troops. He desperately needed weapons and accessories, since the French had seized all that they could to leave the population unarmed. The Portuguese army was being re-formed and would need uniforms for 40,000 infantrymen and 8,000 cavalrymen. Such huge demands were due to a general and spontaneous mobilization everywhere in the country. All the old regular, militia and 'Ordenanza' were rising again, and there was every challenge imaginable associated with reorganizing an army. However, unlike in late 1807, everyone in Portugal had experienced the bitter taste of a brutal occupation and there was no question that a fight to the death was the only viable option. On their part, the British were most attentive to Ambassador de Souza's call for help. They tried to send what they could immediately, and muster troops to send to Portugal and Spain.

INITIAL STRATEGY

Repression and reaction

The fortress at Elvas, one of the pillars of French security in the west of Spain. (Anne S.K. Brown Military Collection, Brown University Library, Providence, USA)

It can be debated whether there was any British, Portuguese, Spanish or French grand strategic plan in the summer of 1808 and for sometime thereafter. The news reaching England of the widespread uprisings in Spain and Portugal showed that something had gone very wrong with Napoleon's ambitious plan to annex the Iberian Peninsula. Pleas for military help were coming in from Spanish and Portuguese patriots and British officials at Gibraltar did what they could to supply arms and equipment.

The immediate French strategy in Portugal was to ruthlessly suppress any uprising by sending out strong columns from its three main bases: Lisbon and the fortresses of Elvas and Almeida. But the Portuguese patriots turned out to be quite resilient. On 20–22 June, Gen Francisco de Silveira, at the head of a motley levy, defeated Gen Loison's French regular force marching towards Porto at Teixeira and Paseo de Regua; the French force retreated; the great fortress of Almeida was surrounded by thousands of Portuguese, and the north was basically freed. However, the French army had also been busy suppressing the uprisings in central and southern Portugal with wanton brutality. For instance, on 29 July, the city of Evora was carried by storm by Gen Loison's troops. The attack degenerated into horrific scenes of French soldiers pursuing and bayoneting harmless old men, women, children and babies in a mad, blood-filled frenzy. The slaughter was great; any inhabitants, especially women, who could not escape were outraged and often put to the sword. French accounts mention losing 100 killed and 200 wounded and killing 3,000 to 4,000 Portuguese and Spaniards besides taking 4,000 prisoner – but the true figure will likely never be known. This was, of course, something of a sinister strategy by French generals to terrorise the people into submission. It may have been the worst mistake they made during the Peninsular War. Instead of weakening, the people were now driven by a desire for revenge, as unfortunate French stragglers soon found out.

The surrender of Gen Dupont's French army at Baylen, southern Spain, 19 July 1808. Not only was the French force defeated, it was totally lost to Gen Castanos's Spanish army. The news of this disaster startled the world; until then, the French army seemed invincible on the battlefields. (Painting by Casado del Alisal. Collection and photo: Museo del Prado)

General Francisco de Silveira, c. 1815. Later awarded the title of Count of Amarante, his memory remains revered as a hero of the Peninsular War by his countrymen. Since he was rather independent-minded, he was not appreciated very much by Gen Wellesley and his staff so that he has remained somewhat unknown for his qualities in British histories. Yet he played a decisive role in the defence of northern Portugal. (Period engraving. Private collection. Author's photo)

Meanwhile all of Spain was ablaze. The force of about 55,000 French troops there found itself suddenly set upon from all sides. Napoleon's pressures on the Spanish royal family had produced the abdication of King Carlos IV; his eldest son, Fernando, was then quietly put under house arrest in France. Napoleon's brother Joseph was then proclaimed 'King of Spain and the Indies'. Far from settling the issue, this outraged nearly every Spaniard; the popular feeling to save the nation was to rally in defence of their legitimate monarch, King Fernando VII. Thus, even though he remained interned in a French château until 1814, Fernando VII was the symbol who rallied the nation.

Later in July 1808 came news of the battle of Baylen in Andalucia. There, on 19 July, Gen Pierre Dupont's 24,000-strong French army met a Spanish army of 29,000 men, led by Gen Francisco Castaños. The French force had not only been defeated, it was destroyed. Only a few thousand French troops had escaped, some 2,600 were killed or wounded, and an astounding 17,635 surrendered. This was incredible news in the context of 1808. Napoleon's French army had seemed invincible, but the Spanish had now proven that even a large French imperial force could be not merely defeated, left to fight another day, but totally wiped out. Baylen would become the symbolic rallying cry for all those who opposed Napoleon's rule in Spain and throughout Europe.

Appraised of these events in the Peninsula, Britain at last saw a gap in Napoleon's 'Fortress Europe' and devised a loosely formulated strategy of its own: it rushed an expeditionary force of 8,700 men from England under Maj-Gen Arthur Wellesley, later to become the Duke of Wellington. It landed at Figueira da Foz in Portugal, and from 1 August was joined by another 5,400-strong contingent from Gibraltar. Under the competent British general, who had learned much of his trade in India and revealed himself to be a most remarkable tactician, the force moved south towards Lisbon and the main French army. Wellesley's army was joined by many Portuguese levies under Gen Freire, but these had few weapons and were often unfamiliar with military manoeuvres; thus, the brunt of the action would be borne by British troops. In Lisbon meanwhile, Gen Junot was trying to assemble as many men as he could to march north and engage Wellesley's army. Gen Delaborde's 4,500-strong French corps was the only force between Wellesley and Lisbon, and he chose to make a stand at Roliça to delay or even stop the British and Portuguese. On 17 August, Wellesley attacked and soon routed Delaborde's troops. On 21 August, Junot was decisively defeated at Vimeiro. After the battle, Wellesley was superseded (due to seniority) by Sir Hew Dalrymple who proceeded to sign the convention of Cintra, allowing the French army to evacuate Portugal. The British now had a solid strategic base on the continent and sent more troops; in December the British army in Portugal, now under the command of the talented Maj-Gen Sir John Moore, numbered some 46,000 men. For its part, the Portuguese army had about 30,000 men at that time, but it faced enormous shortages and lacked good regimental commanders.

Napoleon was not about to accept defeat in Spain and Portugal. He already had diplomatic difficulties, with Austria especially, and felt that this would eventually lead to hostilities – perhaps in the following spring. Therefore, the Iberian problem that had now sprung up had to be settled as soon as possible. At this point, it looked to the world as if he had been utterly defeated there. But in fact, French troops were being reinforced and were regrouping at Vittoria under the leadership of King Joseph and Marshal Jourdain. On 5 November 1808, Napoleon arrived there at the head of some 200,000 men, putting the total strength of his army in Spain at about 300,000 troops. Some of his best marshals were with him: Lannes, Victor, Soult, Ney, Lefebre and Mortier, who were ably assisted by good generals such as Sebastiani, St Cyr and Hugo. All headed south-west and repeatedly defeated the Spanish forces trying to stop them. On 2 December, Napoleon was in sight of Madrid and the Spanish capital surrendered the next day; on 19 December, Barcelona fell and Zaragoza was besieged again.

Still, the British strategy was to strike at the French in Spain. In late November 1808 Sir John Moore, at the head of some 25,000 British troops, marched into Spain with instructions to assist its armies. Everyone was optimistic, filled with visions of liberating Spain. No help from the Portuguese seemed required. However, events were to convince the British of the difficulties of the task.

Having taken Madrid, Napoleon envisioned a move against Lisbon, now that he held most of northern and central Spain. But now Moore's army was in western Spain between Salamanca and Valladolid, threatening Marshal Soult's 2nd Corps; this had to be dealt with at once. Napoleon sent Marshal Ney with his 6th Corps to the rescue, and he himself eventually followed with his Imperial Guard and a strong artillery train. He was fairly sure of reaching the British force and inflicting a terrible defeat upon Great Britain.

Fortunately for the British, Sir John Moore perceived the great danger. Facing the prospect of being squeezed between Soult and Ney's corps, with the Emperor himself coming up with his veteran Guard, Moore concentrated on saving the army. He headed for Corunna, the main port in north-western Spain, where it could be evacuated on British ships. After a harrowing retreat march, the army arrived at Corunna on 11 January 1809, followed by Marshal Soult's corps. On 16 January, the French attacked but did not succeed in breaking the British defensive position, although Sir John Moore was killed in the fighting. Two days later, the last British troops to

The British 26th Regiment of Foot at the battle of Corunna, 16 January 1809. The British managed to repulse the assault of Marshal Soult's troops and evacuate, but Gen Sir John Moore was killed in the battle. (Print after H. Oakes-Jones. Private collection. Author's photo)

embark were on their way back to England. Meanwhile, on 1 January 1809, Napoleon had turned back near Astorga and headed for Paris on urgent news regarding Austria and Russia.

In Lisbon, Maj-Gen Sir John Cradock had succeeded Moore in command of the British army in Portugal. The unfolding events since January 1809 had seemingly discouraged him; he increasingly appeared to believe that any success in the Peninsula was hopeless. Far from thinking of an aggressive strategy to hamper the French and help his allies, Cradock was becoming convinced that the only course of action to save his 20,000 men lay in the evacuation of the entire force from Portugal. This almost incredible strategy was already being articulated when he ordered the British contingent at Almeida to regroup in Lisbon, thus leaving Portugal's citadel in the north-east largely undefended.

But in Almeida, there was also a new unit of green-coated soldiers. They were largely Portuguese, although a few British officers had senior command, and indeed the corps had initially been organized in England a few months earlier. It was, by comparison with other Portuguese units, well armed, well equipped and well disciplined.

The Loyal Lusitanian Legion

Although short-lived, this was a truly outstanding unit that came about during extraordinary times in the history of the Peninsular War as well as in Portugal's struggle to retain its independence. It is, of course, central to the story of the operations regarding Alcantara, to the extent that it probably

Privates of the Loyal Lusitanian Legion, 1808–1811. Since it was a corps of light troops that began its organization in England, dark green was the colour chosen for its uniform (up to 1807, Portuguese light troops wore sky blue and later brown), which was in line with British army practices. It was made by the military clothiers firm of Pearse in England. The men's coatee was trimmed with white cord and lace. The facing colours at the cuffs and collar were dark green for the light infantry and riflemen, black for the artillery detachment and white for the light cavalry. There were some supply difficulties, but, on the whole, the legion may have been the best-uniformed unit in the Portuguese army up to about the summer of 1809. Grey jackets were also procured as undress and, in later 1809, seemed to have been the only such garments left to some men. The weapons were British and inspected as 'in tolerable serviceable order' and 'good and serviceable' in January 1810. The muskets were surely of the India Pattern model. The 120 rifles sent to the legion in 1808 would have been Baker's with sword bayonets and this indicates that the original scheme called for six riflemen in each company of the original establishment. (Plate by William Younghusband, © Osprey Publishing)

Sir Robert Wilson, colonel of the Loyal Lusitanian Legion, 1808–1811. This 1818 print after H.W. Pickersgill shows Sir Robert in the uniform of a major-general. His services in foreign armies is denoted by the many orders and medals awarded by Austria, Prussia and other German states, Russia, Turkey and Portugal. (Collection and photo: National Historic Sites, Parks Canada)

could not have been done without this unit. It is therefore essential at this point to delve into the history of this remarkable corps. It had an unusual origin, as the unit was actually mooted by Portuguese expatriates in England. It also called upon a few British officers and gunners to become the cadre of its Portuguese officers, NCOs and enlisted men.

In the summer of 1808, the Chevalier de Souza, Portugal's ambassador in London, was a very busy man. Not only was he successfully lobbying the British government for all sorts of military and material help, he had even proposed 'that 3 battalions should be formed with a company of artillery' to serve in Portugal. This initiative came from Portuguese refugees who had fled their country following the French occupation in late 1807. Most were now in southern England and, upon learning of the uprisings in Spain and

Portugal, they enlisted the support of Ambassador de Souza to raise such a unit. He in turn brought the proposal to the British government, the only body then able to finance and organize such a corps. While it was acknowledged that senior command would go to British officers, there were Portuguese officers of experience among the refugees, ready to take up arms in the proposed corps. The unit would initially be raised from 'the Portuguese in England of which there are about 400 exclusive of officers [who] should form a battalion. That the cloathing of a whole battalion with arms and accoutrements &c should be immediately expedited to Plymouth ... clothing for the two other battalions should be made up at Oporto ... two light field pieces and one howitzer should be put on board ... if Lord Castlereagh approves the project...' On 29 July 1808, Lord Castlereagh approved on behalf of the British government the 'proposal for raising and arming a Corps of Portuguese' and gave 'the necessary directions for providing clothing and accoutrements ... [with] ... arms & field pieces that may be required' for the new corps (WO 6/164).

As can be seen, the material considerations were important to the Portuguese who were totally deficient in such essential supplies. On 1 August 1808, even before officers were appointed and enlistment in England began, a requisition went out to Treasury for 2,302 uniforms complete with accoutrements. At about the same time, another requisition was made for weapons, namely 2,070 muskets with bayonets, 120 rifles with bayonets, 64 pistols, 24 bugles, 24 drums, 12 axes, 12 saws and 316 swords. The high number of swords was because 'corporals in the Portuguese service carry swords as well as muskets'. The artillery would have four light 4-pounder guns and two light howitzers with ammunition in proportion (WO 6/172; FO 63/67).

Command of the Legion would go to one of the flamboyant *beau sabreur* personalities of the Napoleonic wars, Sir Robert Wilson. As a young officer in the 1794 campaign in Flanders, Sir Robert gained lasting fame by saving the Austrian emperor, Francis I, from being captured by the French. A daring and brave officer, he further distinguished himself in the 1799 Helder campaign in Holland, in Egypt during 1801 and at the Cape of Good Hope in 1806. He was also skilled with a pen and wrote a popular account of the Egyptian campaign followed by an essay on improvements to military organization, in which he called for the abolition of corporal punishment in the army. This made him known and appreciated in political and government circles, where he proved to be a smooth courtier-soldier. He obviously had a very engaging personality, was most active, full of charm, enterprising and quite shrewd. From late 1806, he was trusted and employed by the Secretary of State for Foreign Affairs, George Canning, as a special envoy to Prussia and to Russia. He thus was present at the great battles of Eylau (6–7 February 1807) and Friedland (14 June) as a British officer attached to the Russian and Prussian general staff organizations. He was also an outstanding secret agent, and later managed to warn Canning about Russian intrigues. These activities near the pinnacle of power unfortunately went to his head and, in time, would be his undoing. In 1808

Maj-Gen Arthur Wellesley, later Duke of Wellington, c. 1812. Certainly one of the greatest tacticians and strategists of his times, he wears the dress uniform for generals with the aiguillette introduced from 1 July 1811. (Contemporary portrait. Museo Napoleonico, Havana. Author's photo)

Sir Robert was haunting the corridors of power and, on 4 August, he was given command of the Loyal Lusitanian Legion with the rank of colonel.

The legionnaires were to be 'under Portuguese officers and sent to Portugal' but there were several British officers appointed. They eventually were, besides Wilson, lieutenant-colonels William Mayne, Frederick, Baron de Eben, Edward Hawkshaw, Major John Grant, captains James Nesbitt Charles, John Scott Lillie, Charles Western and Edward Baron Daubraya, surgeons Mellingen and Bollman, and Cadet John Russel. The new unit was to be organized and sent to Portugal as soon as possible. It was a tall order to recruit, organize and train a corps in very little time, but a challenge that Wilson took up with energy and spirit. On 12 August he was already asking for an additional list of articles to be provided for his unit. He also felt there should be some cavalry attached to it. In his view, a legionary corps should have cavalry as well as infantry and artillery, a perception initially shared also by Ambassador de Souza. It was around this time that the name 'Loyal Lusitanian Legion' was coined.

The legion's establishment called for a staff of 38 officers and NCOs, three light infantry battalions with eight companies per battalion, each company having 97 officers and men for a total of 2,328, plus the artillery company with 86 officers and men. Later on, a light cavalry component was indeed added to the legion. However, there was no question of raising nearly 3,000 men in England. Even a single battalion of 776 officers and men would not be feasible; however, if at least an embryo and the cadre for one battalion with the Legion's basic staff could sail for Portugal, it would be great encouragement to the Portuguese. It was obviously felt by Ambassador de Souza that Porto would be the best place for the legion 'under the auspices of the Venerable Bishop of Oporto'. Within about six weeks, they were on their way and Sir Robert and his men were in Porto by October.

The organization of the legion continued there and, by 4 November 1808, Sir Robert Wilson could report that 'Major General Beresford has inspected the Legion under my command'. Sir Robert stated that 'drilling of the men has not been so much our first object, as the establishment of an interior economy' but discipline had 'been completely attained'. The men were formed 'according to the British regulations' which meant 'putting into the Portuguese language the necessary instructions' of British light infantry drill and other regulations. The recruits were to be at least 'about 5 feet 3 inches' and General Beresford ordered the 1st Battalion to be completed as soon as possible. The artillery company was 'now complete and well disciplined in gunnery, the greater part being old soldiers' from England. The formation of the cavalry component was delayed until 'the infantry were completed' except for a few mounted 'men required after orderly and other necessary duty' (WO 1/417).

Sir Robert had appointed Major William Mayne as lieutenant-colonel commanding the 1st Battalion and hoped 'to insinuate many British officers to join the corps so as to establish a perfect system of organisation' along British lines. In the meantime, he found the recruited Portuguese men 'everything that I could wish, and the officers, very willing and zealous'. The majority of the officers were Portuguese. By December, Lt-Col Mayne reported the legion at 'between two and three thousand men, and they might have been extended to ten thousand men or to more! but the finances of Portugal then shrank from such increase. Numerous recruits were rejected daily' as a result.

Relations between Sir Robert and the Bishop of Porto were not especially smooth. The bishop and his officers felt that the legion was an integral part of the army that they were mustering in the north of Portugal and that it should be under their authority. Sir Robert, who corresponded freely with senior ministers in the British cabinet, obviously felt that his unit was something of a semi-official extension of the British forces in Portugal, and should not be tampered with by inexperienced Portuguese clerics and officers of doubtful ability. He wanted a free hand to do as he wished and did not especially want the close scrutiny of senior commanders. Wilson thus thanked the bishop and his staff officers for their concerns, went his own way, completed the 1st Battalion and appointed as lieutenant-colonel of the 2nd Battalion the Baron de Eben, formerly aide-de-camp to the Prince of Wales, who went to Coimbra to start its organization and recruitment in that area. In all this, the legion's senior officers were resolute in their objective: create a first-rate light corps that could raid, confuse and upset an enemy much superior in numbers and resources; in effect, the Napoleonic version of a commando unit.

4 NOVEMBER 1808

Loyal Lusitanian Legion inspected for the first time

The fortress of Almeida. This fortress guarded the access to north-eastern Portugal. It formed an ideal base for raiders into Spain in early 1809. (Old photo print. Private collection. Author's photo)

Recruiting and training went on until early December 1808 'when, according to Lt-Col Mayne's account, after a notice of only thirty-six hours, the Legion's 1st battalion marched from Oporto, by order of Lieutenant-General Sir John Cradock, with the intention of proceeding to Villa Real, and defending (as far as this force might defend) the approach to the northern provinces of Portugal'. The unit thus assembled on 13 December, was inspected by the Bishop of Porto who 'walked along the ranks, and with reason praised their handsome appearance'. The next day Sir Robert Wilson and about 800 men marched out amidst many cheers and 'vivas' from Porto's population, Harriet Slessor and friar do Sao Carlos observing that 'with drums beating and colours flying, they marched out of the town, all appearing, officers as well as men, in high spirits'.

The best possible place to defend the Portuguese border was the fortress of Almeida rather than Vila Real, and it was there that Sir Robert took the Loyal Lusitanian Legion. Almeida, which had about 2,000 inhabitants, was the key to penetrating Portugal in the north-east. It guarded one of the two main passes through the mountains that separated Spain from Portugal (the other pass was further south and guarded by the fortress of Elvas). Almeida was built on a slight plateau at the foot of hills and small rivers that extended westward into Portugal. To the east were the plains of Leon in Spain, and the Spanish fortified city of Ciudad Rodrigo lay only 35km away. It could be seen in the distance, sitting on the plains it guarded.

Historically, Ciudad Rodrigo had been Spain's sentry in case of attacks from Portugal, but this had not occurred for a century and its fortifications, while redoubtable, were not outstanding. Almeida was something else. Possibly the most formidable fortress in both northern Portugal and Spain, it could stand a prolonged siege by a large force if defended by a resolute garrison. On the flat and rocky plateau where it was built, it commanded the highest ground for many kilometres around and was a main crossroads, thus making it commercially viable. As a result, Almeida was always part of the strategic planning for any conflict involving Portugal. Its old castle dated from the early 14th century. The fortress, much of which can still be admired today, was commissioned by King Joao IV, beginning in 1641. It was designed by a French engineer, Antoine Deville, and featured the latest trends in fortifications design. The Spanish attacked several times, hoping to stop its construction, but all their attempts failed. In 1663, the Spanish suffered a crushing defeat there, confirming Portugal's independence as a separate kingdom.

Improvements continued to be made to its works in the following decades, but in 1762 it fell to Spanish and French troops, its loss due to its 81-year-old commander's lack of resolve rather than any defect in its fortifications. Restored to Portugal in 1763, additional works and batteries were built to render it more formidable. Occupied briefly by the French until September 1808, it was now guarded by Portuguese levies and British troops. Large quantities of British supplies, worth £150,000 and intended for Sir John Moore's army, were safely stored in the fortress. The Bishop of Porto had given positive orders for Sir Robert not to lead his troops into

Spain, but to stay at the border and defend it at all costs. But the Bishop was not a soldier and Sir Robert had other, more martial ideas.

From a tactical point of view, Almeida could form an ideal base of operations for a force to cross into Spain. This is what Sir Robert Wilson immediately saw once he reached the fortress. He was greeted by the British 45th and 97th Regiments, which formed the essential part of the garrison at this important fortress. Its governor was Lt-Col William Guard of the 45th, and the senior commanding officer was Brig-Gen Cameron. Thus, with this respectable force, the great fortress was certainly secure from anything except a major attack requiring two or even three French army corps. As the French were preoccupied elsewhere, this was quite unlikely. Almeida therefore looked secure and Sir Robert could moot schemes to tickle what French troops there were in western Leon.

THE PLAN

A retreat?

A plan of sorts was starting to emerge as Wilson and his officers, especially Lt-Col Mayne, looked east from the walls of Almeida at the rolling plains of Spain. Here was surely an opportunity to hinder French communication lines between the French corps of marshals Soult and Ney in the north and those of Marshal Victor in the south. According to Spanish and Portuguese partisans, there were few French troops between the cities of Salamanca and Merida. The strategic points in between these cities were the pass through the

28

Sierra de Gata mountains about 60km south of Ciudad Rodrigo, the pass at Puerto de Banos about 60km due east of the Gata pass and, further to the south-west, the town of Alcantara on the upper Tagus.

Alcantara was at a crossroad on the only fairly direct road between Ciudad Rodrigo, Salamanca and Merida. Access to Madrid via Coria and Talavera de la Reina was also possible by using the main road going east.

18 JANUARY 1809

Last British troops are evacuated from Corunna

French foot artilleryman in cold weather marching order, Spain, c. 1808–1809. In late 1808, Napoleon committed some 300,000 men to subdue Spain. Those chasing Sir John Moore's British army through Galicia often faced snow storms. (Watercolour by Pierre Albert Leroux. Anne S.K. Brown Military Collection, Brown University Library, Providence, USA. Author's photo)

Furthermore, Alcantara was also at the start of a difficult mountain road – a path at times – that crossed into nearby Portugal and led to the city of Castello Branco. As already discussed, Alcantara was famous for its ancient order of knights and its imposing Roman bridge. Both of these were born of its exceptional strategic location, in the days before railways and four-lane superhighways could bypass the town.

The communications infrastructure in the Iberian Peninsula at the time of the Napoleonic Wars was inadequate even by the standards of that time. Indeed, it was a subject on which both the French and the British agreed upon as they both grappled with the challenges of moving troops and their supplies on Iberian roads, such as there were. The local inhabitants routinely used mules for transporting supplies, and after a while the French and British armies adjusted to this mode of transport. So, by using mules, supplies could follow a body of light troops that would move swiftly across the plains and mountains. Horsed soldiers might be best in the flatter landscape, but, apart from the plains of Leon, the terrain was often full of hills south of Ciudad Rodrigo and several *sierras* also extended east as far as the Escorial – the palace and church built by King Felipe II during the 16th century, situated only 40km northwest of Madrid.

To Wilson and his officers, these geographical conditions could make an ideal terrain in which to deploy their light infantry corps. The flatter topography would prove a challenge and a real danger if the area was patrolled by sizeable bodies of French cavalry. On the other hand, it would have to be a markedly superior cavalry force with strong hitting power because the men of the Loyal Lusitanian Legion were also trained to fight cavalry as British infantry would. As for French line infantry columns, they moved no faster than other armies and it was expected that they could be outpaced by the legionnaires.

While there was no precise plan to hit any specific target, the conditions were right for a vigorous foray eastward. For adventurous and keen leaders looking for action, and (why not) some glory too, the opportunity was there for the taking. An aggressive stance and drive into Spain would have all sorts of benefits. The greatest one was that it would upset the French and, with some luck, divert their attention from their overwhelming priority of subduing northern Spain, where Sir John Moore's army was. No one in Portugal then knew that Sir John's army was in full retreat, trying to reach Corunna before the French could catch it.

Surely, the British thought, the Spanish patriots in Leon and northern Estremadura would be encouraged to see allied troops again roaming in their midst so soon after Moore's quite remarkable foray and they could be counted upon for good information as well as some material support. The Portuguese too were keen to have a crack at the French outside of Portugal. Thus, morale as well as purely military objectives were favourable to an expedition into Spain, which would blossom into a number of raids in different directions.

On 9 January 1809, all these musings came to an abrupt halt when a courier arrived at Almeida from the British HQ in Lisbon. It brought a message

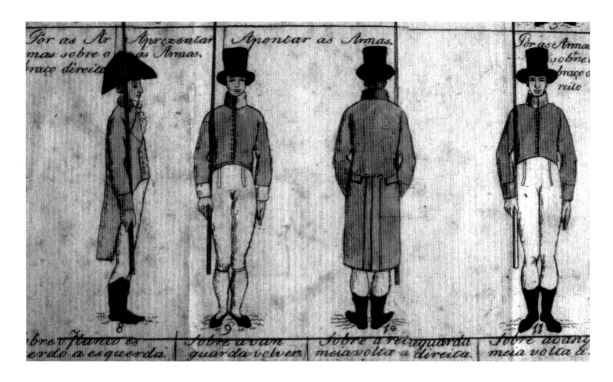

from Sir John Cradock, proving that his own morale was not especially high. Cradock ordered the immediate withdrawal of the 45th and 97th British regiments to Lisbon. He saw his first duty as saving his army in Portugal, which entailed evacuating the country at the first serious alarm that a French invasion force would march on the country. That this attitude potentially left the Portuguese almost helpless against Napoleon does not seem to have had much influence on his attitude.

The 45th and 97th were to join the rest of the army in anticipation of embarking on a fleet that would take the whole British expeditionary force back to Great Britain. This was hardly the plan that Wilson and his British officers had in mind. They had seen themselves roaming the plains of western Spain looking for French targets to hit; instead, they were now invited to leave Almeida along with the British troops and assemble in Lisbon for a possible evacuation.

Apprised of this news, Sir Robert Wilson immediately called a meeting of the British officers of the Loyal Lusitanian Legion. Lt-Col Mayne and Capt Lillie later wrote of the decision that faced them all, once Sir Robert had broken the news of the withdrawal of the British troops from Almeida as well as Gen Cradock's invitation for them to withdraw 'for their own personal safety' and thus leave the legion to its fate. It was left 'at their option either to go or to stay. But they considered that as they then conceived themselves really to be in the service of Portugal, that it would be highly disgraceful at this critical juncture and inconsistent with the character of a British soldier, and with the principles by which their conduct had hitherto been guided, to leave this service; they all consequently determined on not abandoning their brave brethren in arms, but [resolved] to remain and share

Pike drill of Portuguese levies, c. 1808. The Portuguese had been disarmed by the French and had few firearms when the country rose in revolt from June 1808. (Contemporary print. Museu Militar do Porto. Author's photo)

Bandsman, 8th French Line Infantry Regiment, *c.* 1809. French army regimental bandsmen often had colourful uniforms that differed for each unit. In this case, this bass drummer wears the 8th Regiment's sky blue uniform faced with yellow and edged with gold lace. This unit was part of Gen Lapisse's 2nd Division belonging to Marshal Victor's 1st Army Corps and was involved in most actions in and about Alcantara. (Watercolour by Pierre Albert Leroux. Anne S.K. Brown Military Collection, Brown University Library, Providence, USA. Author's photo)

the fate of the Portuguese officers and men whose confidence they had gained and whom they had brought to the frontiers for the purpose of defending their country, well armed and perfectly equipped for active and immediate service.'

Almeida's governor, Lt-Col Guard of the 45th, was to leave with his men. He asked that Lt-Col Mayne of the legion succeed him as governor, at least for the time being, and Sir Robert of course agreed. One can only imagine what the thoughts of the red-coated soldiers were as they marched out of the gates of Almeida and towards Lisbon; or the thoughts of the green-coated officers and men standing on the curtain walls waving them farewell. There were obviously regrets, but it was certainly not a tragic pathos scene. The morale of the men in red and green was quite good, and they remained eager to face the French. For the redcoats, the opportunity would come eventually; for the men in green uniforms, it would be a matter of days.

The British withdrawal notwithstanding, part of the Loyal Lusitanian Legion began moving into Spain under the command of Sir Robert. It consisted of two infantry companies, two of its light guns under Capt Lillie, and its sole squadron of cavalry. Lt-Col Mayne was left in Almeida with a detachment of the legion and some regular Portuguese troops that had been recently reorganized.

As he moved east, elements of Sir Robert's plan were revealed. The idea was to have a loosely posted line of pickets that would gradually extend from Almeida past Ciudad Rodrigo and move further and further east, going past the southern suburbs of Salamanca to Avila and perhaps even as far as the Escorial. This meant that any French troop movements between the Portuguese border and the vicinity of Madrid would very likely be noticed and, depending on its size, might be attacked or harassed. Perhaps due to some luck, Wilson had stumbled upon the one sizeable gap in the French occupation of northern and central Spain. Apart from Andalucia, most of which remained under the realm of the patriots, other areas in Spain might also be without sizeable contingents of French troops, but none of them were within reach of a base such as Almeida, from where one could organize sizeable raids.

This is not to say that the area was barren of French troops. There were over 300,000 French or French-allied troops in Spain. The French forces in central and south-western Spain were substantial. In February 1809, the musters of the French army for effective men-under-arms in their regiments and corps (excluding the sick, wounded or detached) numbered about 28,000 men. They were:

Marshal Victor's 1st Corps (HQ at Merida):
1st Division, Ruffin: 9th Light; 24th and 96th Line (three battalions each): 5,429
2nd Division, Lapisse: 16th Light; 8th, 45th and 54th Line (three battalions each): 7,692
3rd Division, Vilatte: 27th Light; 63rd, 94th and 95th Line (three battalions each): 6,376
Cavalry corps, Beaumont: 2nd Hussars and 5th Chasseurs-à-cheval: 1,386
Westphalian Light Horse: 487
Artillery, 48 guns: 1,523
Staff: 33
Total: 22,926

General Latour-Maubourg's division of reserve cavalry (HQ at Merida): 1st, 2nd, 4th, 9th, 14th and 26th dragoons: 2,527
General Leval's 2nd (German-Dutch) Division: regiments of Holland, Nassau, Baden and Hesse (three battalions each), and Frankforth (one battalion): 3,127. This division was detached from General Sebastiani's 4th Corps posted further east.

Of course, not all of these French troops could drop everything and start chasing after raiders without dire consequences in the sectors they already held secure. But, at a pinch, the French troops could be quickly mustered into a powerful enough field force to cope with the raiders. The most exposed were of course the men of the French 1st Corps, since they were closest to the Portuguese border.

The French had posted garrisons in the various cities and towns – and sometimes the more suspect hamlets – of the area that was now penetrated by a screen of legionnaires. There was, however, a fairly large force in the area of Salamanca: Gen Lapisse's 2nd Division, which had been detached from Gen Victor's 1st Corps further south. Its infantry mustered some

7,600 men fit for duty with, in addition, possibly as many as 16 guns served by some 500 artillerymen. A strong force of dragoons, possibly as many as 1,500, was attached to Lapisse's command. They were probably detached from General Latour-Maubourg's division of reserve cavalry. In their account, Mayne and Lillie mentioned that the French force opposing the legion was about '12,000 of the enemy [that] did maintain their posts in the plains of Salamanca' although the more accurate figure hovers around 9,000 men fit for service.

By mid-January, Wilson and his men were in Ciudad Rodrigo, a city of about 3,000 souls garrisoned by about 1,400 Spanish troops, only 500 of which were regulars. These troops were needed there in case Lapisse's division appeared. British observers had noted with alarm that Spanish troops fired only two volleys a minute compared to the French infantry's three volleys, a fact also noted with satisfaction by French officers. This went a long way towards explaining the frequent defeats of the Spanish.

Trooper of the 1st French Dragoons having a chat with an admiring lady, 1807. The 1st Dragoons was part of General Latour-Maubourg's division of reserve cavalry based in Merida. (Print after Martinet. Anne S.K. Brown Military Collection, Brown University Library, Providence, USA. Author's photo)

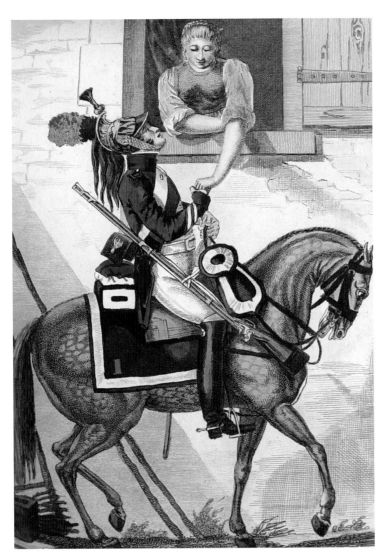

In any event, Loyal Lusitanian Legion soldiers could certainly match the French shot for shot, but Sir Robert's grand plan certainly could not be put into place with merely a few companies, likely numbering fewer than 300 men. The Spanish officers in Ciudad Rodrigo greeted him warmly, but must have smiled at his daring ideas. They might even have thought that he was yet another of these romantic Englishmen who thought that venturing to fight the French in isolated spots of Spain was a little more than a dashing military excursion, something of a martial Grand Tour. But some must have soon heard that he had been skirmishing successfully against the French since the 1790s. Of course, Sir Robert was more of a realist and, as events would prove, a gifted leader of light troops. He knew only too well he did not have enough men, so he gambled. And the stake was no less than the fortress of Almeida. As it was, there might not be enough men – including his

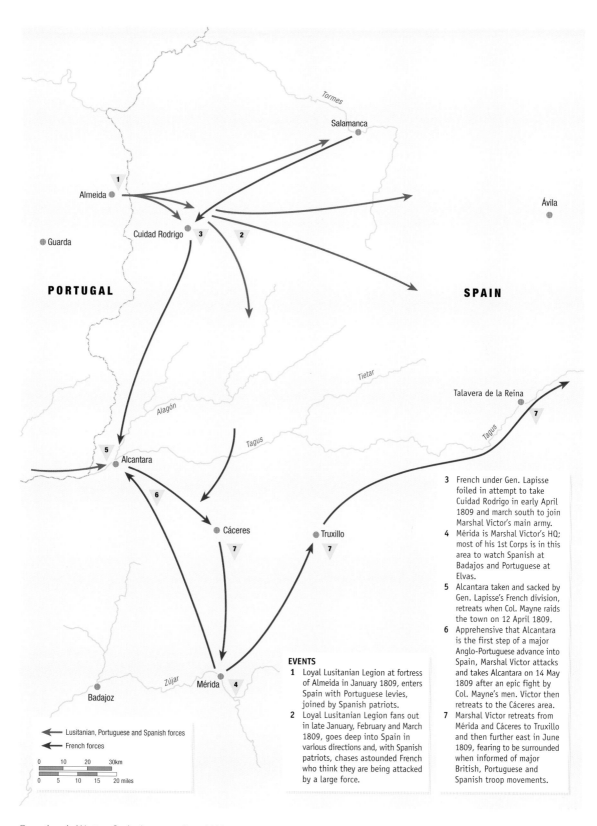

EVENTS

1 Loyal Lusitanian Legion at fortress of Almeida in January 1809, enters Spain with Portuguese levies, joined by Spanish patriots.

2 Loyal Lusitanian Legion fans out in late January, February and March 1809, goes deep into Spain in various directions and, with Spanish patriots, chases astounded French who think they are being attacked by a large force.

3 French under Gen. Lapisse foiled in attempt to take Cuidad Rodrigo in early April 1809 and march south to join Marshal Victor's main army.

4 Mérida is Marshal Victor's HQ; most of his 1st Corps is in this area to watch Spanish at Badajos and Portuguese at Elvas.

5 Alcantara taken and sacked by Gen. Lapisse's French division, retreats when Col. Mayne raids the town on 12 April 1809.

6 Apprehensive that Alcantara is the first step of a major Anglo-Portuguese advance into Spain, Marshal Victor attacks and takes Alcantara on 14 May 1809 after an epic fight by Col. Mayne's men. Victor then retreats to the Cáceres area.

7 Marshal Victor retreats from Mérida and Cáceres to Truxillo and then further east in June 1809, fearing to be surrounded when informed of major British, Portuguese and Spanish troop movements.

Operations in Western Spain, January to June 1809

legionnaires – to defend the fortress if the 2nd French Division appeared or, even worse, Victor or Ney's corps. But these corps were seemingly busy elsewhere and if the 2nd Division could be kept on its toes by his legion, then Almeida and everything around it might be safe.

Sir Robert ordered Lt-Col Mayne to have the British stores removed to a safer location in Portugal as, by now, word was filtering in from the north that Gen Moore's army was crossing Galicia, pursued by a large French force. Once that was done, he was leave a token Portuguese garrison in Almeida and join him with the rest of the legion to beef up the intended line across Leon. In spite of being enormously outnumbered in every quarter, Sir Robert's troops had the stealth and mobility to strike small French parties, and outrun and ambush the pursuit – when the cavalry would come to the rescue.

Another powerful factor was also gaining importance in Spain's isolated landscape: the phenomenal rise of the guerrillas or 'Guerrilleros' that were spontaneously organizing all over Spain. These were partisans whose irregular tactics bordered on those of gangs of highway robbers – the French certainly thought they were bandits. This was largely the result of the excesses and cruelty that French troops subjected the largely defenceless rural populations in many parts of the country. Eventually, some of the men reacted to the soldiers' 'rape and pillage' practices by setting up ambushes; in turn, other French troops would seek revenge by destroying villages and

Don Julian Sanchez, c. 1810. From late 1808, Don Julian's guerrillas basically controlled much of the countryside in Leon. (Contemporary print after a sketch taken from life. Anne S.K. Brown Military Collection, Brown University Library, Providence, USA. Author's photo)

killing indiscriminately. The villagers would escape to nearby mountains and some of them stayed there, watching for the first chance to hit some French patrol and exert a gruesome revenge. By December 1808, the movement had become permanent enough for the Supreme Junta in Sevilla to issue a regulation providing encouragement and instructions to organize guerrilla groups. By April 1809, the Junta was encouraging the 'Land Corsairs,' as the guerrilla bands were termed, 'in the provinces occupied by the French troops, [those] who are capable of bearing arms are authorized to arm themselves, even with prohibited weapons, to attack and loot, on all favourable occasions, the French soldiers, either individually or in groups, to take the food and the supplies intended for their use, in a word, to cause them as much harm and damage as possible'. This was the very definition of guerrilla warfare: total war with little quarter asked or given.

In Leon as elsewhere, Spaniards were anxious to fight the French. However, the vast plains made it more difficult for guerrillas to escape to safety in the hills, and it is likely that early would-be guerrillas were cut down by French dragoons; undisciplined, militarily inexperienced, untrained and badly armed farm workers had no chance against them in a flat landscape. Thus guerrilla bands were scarce in Leon, although some had been seen at Almeida. Then came a former soldier named Julian Sanchez. In early 1809, as French troops were looming into western Spain, Sanchez went off from Ciudad Rodrigo with a dozen mounted men to raid the enemy French. It seems Sanchez decided to do this, as following 'some cruelties exercised on a branch of his family by the French, he took an inveterate hatred to them' according to Costello of the 95th. Sanchez hated the French because they had killed part of his family in cold blood. That cruel slaughter would turn out to be a great misfortune for the French. In time, Sanchez turned out to be one of the best tacticians of mounted guerrilla warfare. His daring cavalrymen, with the smaller bands of Olivera and El Frayle, eventually mustered an estimated 700 men, deployed mostly between Salamanca and Ciudad Rodrigo. There is no evidence that Sanchez met Wilson, but this seems very likely since both were operating in the same area against the same enemy. Spanish levies were said to operate with the legionnaires and the most likely candidates would be Sanchez's men, soon respectfully called 'Don Julian', although he was not a nobleman. Whoever collaborated with the Loyal Lusitanian Legion, they were now spreading out in the landscape and providing invaluable intelligence.

RAIDS IN WESTERN SPAIN

The situation in early 1809 was desperate for Portuguese and British arms. The rumours that Sir John Moore been killed and his army evacuated from northern Spain, while the remaining Spanish troops under Gen La Romana were certain to be annihilated unless they dispersed in the mountains of Galicia, were being confirmed as days and weeks went by. In Lisbon, Sir

Sir John Moore. After marching into Spain from Portugal in November 1808, Sir John's expeditionary force was forced to retreat and evacuate from Corunna in order to save itself. (Anne S.K. Brown Military Collection, Brown University Library, Providence, USA)

John Cradock's only concern seemed to be to sail away with his British army if the French moved towards him. Perhaps the one good thing about his grouping of the British forces at Lisbon was that, in the French view, it created a powerful and concentrated force that might be hard to vanquish – assuming it resisted. In their account, Mayne and Lillie thus related that the 'salvation of Portugal was, at this critical period, in a great measure owing to the enterprising and distinguished services of the Loyal Lusitanian Legion under the British officers; for if the evacuation of the British troops had taken place, a French army of eight or ten thousand men could have marched direct

French line infantry with a regimental colour, 1807. A sergeant-major, distinguished by the two gold stripes above the cuff, holds the colour marked 'Valeur Discipline' (valour and discipline). (Print after Martinet. Anne S.K. Brown Military Collection, Brown University Library, Providence, USA. Author's photo)

to Lisbon, where there could not be collected a regular effective force at that time, of half that number to oppose them'. The French corps in question could easily have been Gen Lapisse's 2nd Division.

Fortunately there were positive elements. Moore's army had been saved and might return one day, while the Legion and its Portuguese and Spanish auxiliaries was roaming about Salamanca in the territory of the French 2nd Division. Indeed, much of this division was 'scattered over the towns in the vicinity of Salamanca, for the purpose of plundering the inhabitants'. Gen Lapisse and his senior officers were starting to get reports of small raids on some of their outposts. This was usual enough in ordinary times, often the work of Spanish peasants taking distant pot-shots at a French patrol. The odd thing in these reports was that the raiders were not the bandit-like rag-tag farmers, but they seemed to be British! They wore good uniforms

Joseph Bonaparte. The elder brother of Napoleon Bonaparte was made King Joseph of Spain in 1808, and abdicated in 1813 after France's defeat at the battle of Vitoria. (Anne S.K. Brown Military Collection, Brown University Library, Providence, USA)

that must have been English (which they were indeed), were well armed, and the officers appeared to speak something else than Spanish or Portuguese – could they be British troops? Perhaps a party of the British army's redoubtable green-coated light infantrymen? If so, this could mean that the British army in Portugal, or part of it, was about to enter Spain and cut communications between Victor's 1st Corps in the south and Ney's 6th Corps further north?

Shortly thereafter came the news of a sharp action at the nearby village of Labobada, whose French garrison had been overrun by a party of green-coated light cavalry led by British officers; a large force of French dragoons had counterattacked and one of the British officers, Lt L'Estrange (originally of the 71st Highland Light Infantry) was captured in the retreat while the rest got away. Actually, his capture was probably fortunate because it strengthened the notion amongst the French staff officers that a British force of unknown size was roaming about.

Then reports came to the French HQ from Ledesma de Tormes further east. This town had been ordered by the French to have cattle and a large sum of money ready to be picked up or else the town would be destroyed. Now it was occupied by a party of these new, well-uniformed enemy troops. It must have been even more puzzling to be told that, unlike British skirmishers, they were all mounted. The Legion's account provides the explanation: the infantrymen were 'mounted on all sorts of mules and horses that could be procured' to accompany its cavalrymen. The town's 'ransom' of money, horses and cattle was entrusted to Sir Robert, who sent it under escort to the safety of Ciudad Rodrigo, while leaving a receipt with his signature for the amount of cash, horses and cattle entrusted. The French, enraged at such daring, sent a strong force from Salamanca to Ledesma to carry out their threat if the ransom was not paid. Instead, the town's leading official handed them the receipt signed by Sir Robert Wilson! This unsettling document had the desired effect on the startled French officers, and the town was not looted nor destroyed. However, the French left a garrison there when the main body returned to Salamanca. In fact, elements of the Legion were still nearby, undetected and watching Ledesma. One night, under the command of Lt-Col Grant, they attacked the French soldiers at their advanced posts 'and surprised them sitting round their fires in the woods, by falling on them suddenly, and killed or dispersed the whole'. Thereafter, the French kept to 'within the walls of the place'.

Such acts were surely repeated many times. However, Mayne and Lillie's account appears to be the only well-known account of the legionnaires' many raids that were carried out during the first months of 1809. But even it does not usually give dates or much details on the actions; they are often mentioned almost in passing as one raid leads to another, the number of men engaged is usually not mentioned, and neither, in most cases, are the officers' names. It is now next to impossible to even know the week or even the month when the event occurred, and details are minimal. It is also obvious that many engagements were not recorded. On the other hand, one thing is certain: there were a lot of raids and they were obviously carried out

OVERLEAF: Loyal Lusitanian Legion surprises French troops, 1809

Although the background here is the superb San Benito Monastery, seat of the Order of the Knights of Alcantara, this type of scene occurred dozens of times in Spanish villages and small towns going from the Portuguese border to as far east as the area of the Escorial, close to Madrid. No relatively isolated French detachment was safe from such raids from January to May 1809, first on the wide-ranging plains of Leon and later in Estremadura, especially along the Portuguese border. Information is vague on the raids, but these can be interpreted as the Napoleonic version of commando raids; they were performed by well trained, well equipped, well led regular Portuguese soldiers who were obviously the elite of their army. The senior officers were British and they imparted a fighting doctrine that was an outstanding success, thanks also to the Spanish guerrillas that cut off communications between French corps. The French were far more numerous, the odds being possibly nine or ten to one, but could never catch the raiders and, at one point, thought they were part of a mythical 12,000 strong Anglo-Portuguese army…!

on the spur of the moment if conditions looked favourable. This followed the basic plan to alarm the French as much as possible. 'Scarcely a day passed without some enterprise of this nature [a raid on some French outpost] occurring, which tended most considerably to the annoyance of the enemy, never permitting them a moment's tranquillity, and it likewise did not suffer them to scatter small plundering parties over the country, never knowing when and where they might expect to be attacked.' Such results would have been impossible without the well-acknowledged 'assistance of the Spanish guerrillas, and from the attachment and fidelity manifested by the native peasantry, who bore an inveterate enmity towards the French on all occasions'.

The morale of the French soldiers – conscripts for the most part, taken to an alien land where they were detested – was not always as grand as Napoleon's bulletins to his army made it sound. Desertion was always a problem, and it was heartily encouraged by the legionnaires 'in consequence of hand-bills circulated' amongst the French soldiers telling them they would be protected and taken to a safe place if they absconded. It seems many did.

Another type of disruption suffered by the French was the interception of items sent by Napoleon to his brother King Joseph, including dispatches, luxuries such as butter, and the royal seals of office of his new government. The guerrillas were especially good at intercepting couriers and they would pass the dispatches to Sir Robert and his officers; many of them had a gentleman's education and could read French as well as question dispatch riders (or at least those who had not been put to the sword by their guerrilla captors). Thus they learned, along with the latest news from Paris in various gazettes, that Gen Lapisse believed the forces harrying them to be an Anglo-Portuguese corps of up to some 12,000 men! The French lack of reliable information was of course due to their abysmal relations with the Spanish, the result of wanton pillaging and killings; in return, the Spanish did everything they could to keep them in the dark or provide them with misinformation. Thus, the staff officers of the 2nd French Division were convinced, for instance, that Ciudad Rodrigo and Almeida had sizeable garrisons.

As it was, news of the Loyal Lusitanian Legion's exploits were reaching Gen Cradock, but the British staff with him seemed to think that the legion was doomed. On 20 January 1809, it was learned in Lisbon that 'Sir Robert Wilson [was] very critically situated occupying a

Marshal Nicolas Soult, *c*. 1809. Nicolas Jean-de-Dieu Soult became a marshal in 1804 and duke of Dalmatia in 1808. (Print after Pierre-Louis de Laval. Private collection. Auntor's photo)

pass on the Aguada [River], almost 3 leagues below Ciudad Rodrigo' and that he was 'wholly unsupported, nor has been advised … to fall back, and from information [he received] he imagines that Sir John Moore is withdrawing his troops through Galicia'. The enemy, estimated at about 7,000 strong in Lisbon, was reported 'within 11 leagues of him' (WO 1/232). As seen above, Wilson was in fact well supported by the Spanish, knew that Sir John Moore's army would be aided by any disturbances that he could create in Leon, was not critically pursued by the French and, undaunted, went ever deeper into Spain – getting within six miles (9.6km) of Salamanca. Meanwhile, Lt-Col Mayne and part of the legion had been sent to the pass at Banos, southeast of Ciudad Rodrigo, to intercept any French movements.

If even the British were unsure where Wilson and his legionnaires were, it was truly a grand riddle for the French. They did not know which way to turn, since the new and mysterious force kept appearing in unexpected places. So far it had been mainly in the area between Ciudad Rodrigo and Salamanca. But things were about to get even more complicated. With the British force that had been pursued in Galicia having now been evacuated, Marshal Soult's 2nd Corps was now master of north-western Spain with no viable Spanish opponents. Marshal Ney's 6th Corps was moving further west in Galicia.

Soult moves on Portugal

In Paris, Napoleon had meanwhile devised a strategy to invade Portugal. Marshal Soult's corps would invade from the north, Gen Lapisse's division would move into the centre and Marshal Victor's 1st Corps would attack the south. It looked great on a map, but Victor had to watch Spanish activity in Andalucia, to his southern flank, because Gen Cuesta's army was known to be in the area. He also had to face the fortresses of Badajos and Elvas to the west. With only 9,000 men, Gen Lapisse's 2nd Division was too weak to attempt any grand operations against Ciudad Rodrigo and Almeida; indeed, Victor wanted the division, which properly belonged to his corps, to join the rest of his army in Estremadura. When pressed about Napoleon's orders by Marshal Jourdain, he answered that he could not accomplish anything further without more troops. That Gen Lapisse was now reporting being set upon by some 12,000 enemy troops, some of whom appeared to be British – not the despised Spaniards or Portuguese – was even more unsettling. Indeed, Gen Lapisse had tried to send a detachment to Marshal Victor, but it had been turned back by the mysterious force at the pass of Banos. The result was that communications were all but cut off between Lapisse and Victor. Under these circumstances, the two Frenchmen viewed any move into Portugal by either of them was quite unrealistic. Had the French known the disarray of Gen Cradock, the puny British force of only some 19,000 effective men, the hopeless situation of the Portuguese army and the true numbers of Sir Robert's legion, they could have easily marched into a collapsing Portugal. As it was, and according to the information available, only Marshal Soult's 40,000 troops had a viable chance of success. Ney's 6th Corps would occupy Galicia while Soult would attack northern Portugal.

In 1809, Marshal Soult was rated as one of Napoleon's best tacticians and probably one of the most respected soldiers in the Imperial army. As such, he was somewhat senior to some other marshals and he acted as such. That did not always result in harmonious relations, notably with Ney. Victor acknowledged him, but usually went his own way when he could; this was the case in early 1809. Soult also had a secret ambition in Portugal, to be crowned king of Northern Lusitania – a title he hoped would be created by Napoleon, once Portugal was occupied for good and partitioned. As Marshal Murat had already been crowned king of Naples, Soult had great hopes that if he could secure at least part of Portugal his dream might come true – a powerful incentive to execute Napoleon's invasion plan successfully. Now that Moore's army was out of Corunna, Soult moved to the Atlantic coast and, on 28 January, took the Spanish naval bases of Ferrol, Vigo and Tuy and regrouped.

French infantryman in Spain playing a guitar, c. 1809. His red epaulettes and shako decorations reveal him to be an elite grenadier as well as a music fan. He is most likely recently arrived from France because he is wearing a complete regulation uniform. Many of the soldiers conscripted from the southern departments bordering the Pyrenees with Spain knew guitar music and some were also fluent in Spanish or Catalan. (Watercolour by Pierre Albert Leroux. Anne S.K. Brown Military Collection, Brown University Library, Providence, USA. Author's photo)

Due to the arduous pursuit of Moore's army, posting garrisons and campaigning in wintry Galicia (a colder region of Spain), many thousands of Marshal Soult's soldiers were sick or unfit for duty, and his available field force to move on to Portugal was only about 22,000 men. But as he correctly estimated, it was quite enough. The Portuguese levies may have been numerous, but the French intelligence reports concluded that they, as a whole, were badly armed and worse disciplined. What few better-armed troops there were could not form much of an opposition, and there seemed to be no British troops in northern Portugal. In early March, Marshal Soult crossed into Portugal heading for Porto via the Tamega valley. The only somewhat organized force was Gen Silveira's 10,000 men, a ragged command at best, part of which tried to defend the border town of Chaves against Silveira's orders when the French arrived; it was a total fiasco and the place surrendered without a fight.

Braga was next, defended by some 25,000 irregulars who lost all discipline and killed their own Gen Freire when he said they should withdraw. The only fairly regular troops there were a few hundred men of the Loyal Lusitanian Legion that Lt-Col Eben was recruiting and organizing. The Portuguese irregulars then put Eben in command; he knew it was hopeless to try a defence in such circumstances, but was in no position to contradict the mob. The French attacked and quickly

Private, Voltigeur Company, 16th Light Infantry, c. 1808–1812. The 16th was part of Gen Lapisse's 2nd Division of Marshal Victor's 1st Army Corps. As such it was often the opponent of the Loyal Lusitanian Legion's forays into Spain in early 1809, took part in the horrid sack and rape of Alcantara and was part of the forces that were blocked at the Roman bridge.
(Watercolour by Pierre Albert Leroux. Anne S.K. Brown Military Collection, Brown University Library, Providence, USA. Author's photo)

overcame the defences, then swept through town, bayoneting anything that moved. Only Eben and his legionnaires managed an orderly withdrawal. Confusion and disorder were rampant in Porto and some of the garrison's officers lacked confidence. Nevertheless some stubborn resistance was given by detachments of the legion, but Soult's troops finally took the city amidst considerable slaughter and drowning of civilians on 29 March. Lt-Col Eben with remnants of the legion managed to escape south with other Portuguese troops.

Into Estremadura

So far, much of Estremadura had not been the scene of much action. In a sense, it had been spared due to the Loyal Lusitanian Legion's ongoing raids in Leon. True, its south-eastern part was still occupied by Marshal Victor's 1st Corps, but there had been no actions or alarms of the sort that Gen Lapisse's 2nd Division had been dealing with since January. Victor had to face the static positions at Badajos and Elvas as well as to keep the lid on whatever might come out of Andalucia to the south. Thus he had not stirred while Marshal Soult had descended on northern Portugal, feeling he had hardly enough troops to cope with the potential Spanish and Portuguese threat, by both regulars and guerrillas, as well as the raiders of Leon. Under those circumstances, even a feint toward, say, Badajos could be risky and stir instead a Spanish force to advance from Andalucia. After all, Marshal Victor kept in mind that Gen Cuesta's large Spanish army was on his southern flank.

However, the situation in Estremadura was about to change. Gen Lapisse, who had been supposed to invade Portugal through Almeida was far more anxious to obey his direct superior, Marshal Victor, who had ordered him to bring his 2nd Division down to reunite itself with the main force. The division was down to about 7,000 effective men and thus in no shape to attack fortresses, especially since it did not have a siege artillery train. Still, his opponents, which consisted of Sir Robert's legion detachments and a corps of Spanish irregulars under Don Carlos de España, destined to become a hero of the war, were much too weak to stop him from going south. The only problem was going through the sierra passes; that could become a difficult affair if well defended by the Portuguese and Spanish. Nevertheless, he marched southwards. On 6 April, he arrived within view of Ciudad Rodrigo and sent its governor a summons to capitulate. As expected, he received a defiant answer from the Spanish commander in the city, but Gen Lapisse was a wily officer; by bringing his army there, he would lure Sir Robert into weakening or entirely abandoning the passes that his legionnaires watched, in order to regroup at Ciudad Rodrigo to harass or even engage his French troops. Although he was still not sure of the strength of his enemies, Gen Lapisse was rightly confident that his troops would have few problems repulsing them. Gen Lapisse's gamble worked. Sir Robert took the bait and French scouts soon told Lapisse that the passes – which would have been difficult to cross if fully manned – were all but unguarded. The French division sneaked away by night and, undetected, hurriedly marched south.

When Sir Robert and de España realized the French were no longer near Ciudad Rodrigo, it was too late; they were spotted again going through the pass near Perales. Sir Robert and de España's troops pursued, as did Mayne's command from Banos in the hope of concentrating these forces with levies from the countryside at Perales – where the French might be engaged and stopped. But the French got there first, secured the pass and sacked nearby villages. There was some skirmishing for three days, but Gen Lapisse had no outstanding difficulty and his division went on. He was now heading for the one strategic point on the way: Alcantara.

According to Mayne and Lillie, the legion's detachments under Sir Robert, Lt-Col Grant and Lt-Col Mayne came together at the village of Paio near the pass at Perales and from there 'continued the pursuit of the enemy, uniting all the different bodies for that purpose', which also meant Don Carlos de España's troops and Spanish local levies, and 'pursued the enemy for two days, making a number of prisoners in the different skirmishes with his rear. The pursuit was continued with great success, and harassed the enemy excessively, who supposed they were followed by a large army.' This optimistic account can be tempered by the fact that the 2nd French Division had in fact succeeded in its movement south and probably felt no more harassed by skirmishers in Estremadura than by Lusitanian legionnaires and Don Julian Sanchez's well-organized mounted guerrillas in Leon. Gen Lapisse might have sensed or known there was a force of 'many thousands' following him towards Alcantara, but he also knew they were largely peasants with pitchforks or antiquated firearms that stood not a chance against his 7,000 seasoned regulars.

For all its importance, Alcantara did not have a Spanish garrison. The knights of Alcantara still had their superb convent of San Benito there, but their martial deeds against the Moors during the *Reconquista* were many centuries past; the Order of Alcantara, like all such knightly orders, had become something of a gentlemen's club whose titles were granted to honour notable individuals.

There were probably very few if any knights in Alcantara itself in April 1809. The only other martial force of sorts would have been the town's militia, which could be easily swept away. In terms of fortifications, the medieval walls had partly crumbled. Since the French were coming from the other side of the river Tagus, they had to cross the Roman bridge. To prevent them, 'a kind of abbatis across the road, which had been excavated to the depth of eighteen or twenty feet' was created, which had to be overcome to reach the town. Thus a degree of resistance might be attempted against a weak, unprofessional and unequipped force; Gen Lapisse's division was strong, professional and well-equipped, and could easily carry the place. This must have been the report that scouts brought to Gen Lapisse and his senior officers. Here was a fine opportunity to, at last, let the division's soldiers amass some booty and exact some revenge on the loathed Spanish people, who had been taking aim at them in ambushes for the past months. Besides, the devastation of this strategic town could only hinder the British, Spanish and Portuguese.

Movements of the French army (in blue) and Gen Wellesley and the Anglo-Portuguese army (in red) in northern Portugal, March, April and May 1809. The French under Marshal Soult came down from Galicia (Spain) from the northwest and took Porto on 29 March. Gen Wellesley came from the south and liberated Porto on 12 May. Although the French captured Amarante on 2 May, they had to leave it ten days later and were harassed by Gen Silveira's Portuguese levies until they reached Orense (Spain) on 19 May where Marshal Ney's corps was posted. (Map from Luz Soriano's *Historia da Guerra…* Author's photo)

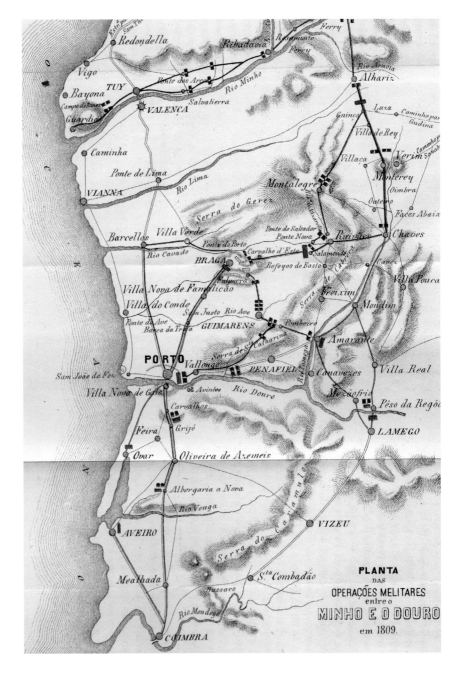

On 12 April, 'the enemy finding himself pressed in his rear' according to Mayne and Lillie (although the author has substantial doubts about that), decided on a frontal assault on Alcantara, combined with a bombardment by the division's field pieces. A strong party of French infantry therefore stormed the abbatis and took it from the hapless town militiamen who tried to defend it, since it was 'unprotected by a regular garrison, or in fact, any military force' – in the sense of trained and well-armed volunteers. Once the Roman bridge was taken, the town was 'cannonaded for some time' by the division's field guns, more French assault troops went to the old walls,

'the gates were forced open' and the French soldiers charged into the streets of Alcantara. What went on next made 12 April 1809, sadly, the blackest day in the town's long history. As the horrified Mayne and Lillie later wrote: 'the revenge and cruelty of the enemy were exercised in the most barbarous manner on the unfortunate and helpless inhabitants who had been found in the town, or taken in endeavouring to effect their escape. They were butchered in the most brutal manner in every direction, and it may be doubted whether the annals of history describe so inhuman a spectacle as that unfortunate place presented on its evacuation by its treacherous and cruel enemy, who performed acts of cruelty and barbarity there that would disgrace the most savage and uncivilized of mankind.'

During the night, even as the rampage in town was ending due to its perpetrators' exhaustion, the shadows of horsemen appeared from the west, within view of the old Roman bridge. This was a party consisting of two squadrons of allied cavalry, one Spanish under Don Carlos de España and one Portuguese, led by Capt Lillie of the legion. They were scouting, but could also conduct a raid if conditions allowed. By early morning of 3 May, Lt-Col Grant had joined them, undoubtedly with a small vanguard of the legion. The French had seemingly not spotted them and did not seem to have posted outer guard parties. Although the French in Alcantara were far stronger, allied scouts ventured closer to the town. They would have quietly ringed the town to perceive what the French were intending to do. Would they make a stand there? Or would they resume their retreat?

The answer eventually came to Lt-Col Grant: the French were leaving Alcantara and marching on the road towards Caceres. Cautiously, the allied soldiers crossed the unguarded Roman bridge, went up the hill road and, seeing no opposition, entered the town. 'The scene witnessed by the above officers, Mayne and Lillie later wrote, exceeds all description; the houses in many parts of this unfortunate place were in flames, and the passage of the streets actually obstructed by mangled bodies of all descriptions lying in heaps; in other places, piles of furniture, and many valuable articles that could not be brought away had been erected in front of houses of some of the principal inhabitants, and had been set fire to, and the mutilated bodies of the unfortunate owners covered with wounds, were thrown on the piles, and there found burning in a most shocking manner... Mixed with human bodies were likewise those of dogs and pigs; in fact, every animal of whatever description the invaders had met with, fell a victim to the unexampled cruelty of those horrid and despicable ruffians; even the chapels, and places of divine worship, did not escape their ravages; they broke open the doors, and polluted the altars of those sacred edifices, carrying off all the plate and valuables they could find; not permitting even the deceased to rest in peace and quietness, they raised the tombstones which form the floors of the cathedrals and other places of worship in these countries, and broke open the coffins, in hopes of being able to discover some hidden treasure that hithertho escaped their search; even the beautiful paintings and scripture pieces which ornament so considerably those magnificent buildings, were mangled and destroyed, and the figures of our Saviour and the Saints, beautifully carved,

12 APRIL 1809

Sack of Alcantara by French troops

as large as life, were knocked about, and mutilated in a most depraved manner.' Thus did the 'unfortunate city of Alcantara ... experience for the first time in these campaigns, the misery and shocking devastation of uncivilized war'.

In the morning, after all that wanton and murderous rampage, the officers and men of the French 16th Light Infantry with the 8th, 45th and 54th regiments of line infantry departed from the town, some undoubtedly carrying all the loot they could march with. Indeed, some of them were seemingly still loitering about at the edge of town, still pilfering the churches and monasteries of whatever gilt there might be by tearing apart exquisitely sculptured altars and columns, a common practice amongst the French troops. No doubt they had a fine time in the beautiful convent of San Benito, drinking what was not destroyed in its cellars, and so, as inferred by some accounts, some French stragglers would have still been around when the allied cavalry entered the town. The French were later said by Wellesley to have been 'forced to evacuate' the town; in fact, the troops forced out would have been parties of stragglers or a rear guard surprised by the Spanish partisans and the Portuguese legionnaires – who would have penetrated the town as a raiding party, infiltrating so as to be able to surprise French detachments still on the spot. There were thus some skirmishes as they came up to places such as the church or the San Benito monastery with stragglers and possibly a rear guard making a hasty retreat to join their army marching away.

The allies' vanguard certainly did not pursue, being far too weak. The best thing to do was to secure the town and its immediate area while waiting for the rest of the allied troops to arrive. Shortly thereafter, small groups of haggard and desperate-looking civilians of all ages and both sexes now appeared at the gates and walked into town. The allied raiders immediately recognized them as the unfortunate townfolk who had saved their own lives by fleeing to the hills. Now, they were back and looking at bodies that they 'recognized, with a good deal of difficulty, by some of their unfortunate families, on their return from the woods and mountains to which they had fled, and the melancholy sadness of these unhappy people, recognizing the mangled bodies of their nearest friends and relations, lying in heaps about the streets, is not to be described'. The scene was forever seared in the memory of Lillie, who wrote those horrified lines, as well as in the unspeakable war memories of all the troopers and legionnaires who entered Alcantara that morning.

It had clearly been previously decided that Gen Lapisse was not to occupy Alcantara – otherwise it would not have been as badly devastated. His orders from Marshal Victor were to join him at Merida. While Alcantara was a very important strategic location, it was practically indefensible – as he had just proven – and thus a bad option, especially as he was shadowed by a numerous enemy force. The pursuers might not be able to attack his division, but he would surely be sealed off by thousands of more-or-less professional enemies, and it would force Marshal Victor to come to the rescue. The better option was to rally Victor's army while guarding his northern flank, and this is what Gen Lapisse was now doing. He arrived at Merida on 19 April.

Change of command

On 22 April 1809, Maj-Gen Sir Arthur Wellesley landed at Lisbon to replace Gen Cradock. The British cabinet had sensed that Cradock's evaluation of the military situation in the Peninsula was too pessimistic. There were opponents of his policy to evacuate without a fight amongst his own staff officers too. Maj-Gen Rowland Hill, who had arrived in Lisbon in early April with 4,000 men, had even managed to convince his superior to allow at least a token advance by the British troops to face Marshal Soult's army. To his credit, Wellesley, while certainly thrilled at assuming command, 'could not reconcile it with his feelings' to replace an officer that he considered to be a successful general. Gen Cradock has since been judged a failure by many historians including the author, but perhaps hastily. He did manage to hold on to most of Portugal with a minimal British force and, apart from the Loyal Lusitanian Legion, very little in the way of a Portuguese force that could have a fighting chance against Napoleon's regulars, who were led by some of that era's most brilliant officers – his superlative generals and marshals. On the other hand, he was not attacked until Marshal Soult's descent upon northern Portugal and, when it occurred, did nothing remarkable to at least hinder the French marshal's army.

Wellesley had hardly arrived before he was deluged with all sorts of political as well as military information, from a variety of more or less reputable sources. His days in India would have trained him to see through fanciful dreams by palace courtiers, intended to please the powers-that-be. Now that he was in Lisbon, Gen Wellesley soon found that most of the information he had received in England was erroneous. Marshal Victor in Estremadura had not been reinforced; Marshal Soult, who had taken Porto on 29 March, had not moved further south, so that the French invasion of Portugal appeared to be stalled. Much of this intelligence was coming from people in the field: guerrillas in Spain and the Portuguese levies that were shadowing the French in northern Portugal. Wellesley had the good sense to value information from humble people as well as from dukes.

The good news for Wellesley was that this intelligence from the field revealed a crucial piece of information: Marshal Soult was not sure where his colleague Marshal Victor was with his army, but it was obvious that he was nowhere near. Indeed, there was every reason to believe the Spanish and Portuguese informants that put Victor and most of his 1st Corps remaining in the area of Merida, in Estremadura. This was quite far from Soult's force in Porto. Furthermore, Gen Lapisse's division, reportedly in the Salamanca area, appeared to be moving south across the plain of Leon towards western Estremadura. Certainly this division was not moving west towards the Douro Valley to attempt to join elements of Soult's army at Amarante. Instead, Sir Robert Wilson and his legionaires were keeping Gen Lapisse on his toes, although Gen Wellesley was likely not quite aware of what was happening in Leon.

For now, Wellesley's priority was to clear the French out of northern Portugal. By appointing him to command and by sending more troops, the British government had committed itself to putting up a fight in the Iberian peninsula. Another important change of command had occurred since March. The Portuguese government was anxious to have a state-of-the-art army with British support and asked the British government to appoint one of its generals to become its commander. The officer chosen by the British government was the 41-year-old William Carr Beresford. A man of great energy, the new marshal of the Portuguese army was not a tactical genius, but he was a gifted military administrator, uncompromising on order and discipline. His efforts at transforming the Portuguese army were shrewd, tireless and most of all, very successful. In all this, as future events would show, the Loyal Lusitanian Legion was left for a time in something of an administrative limbo, since no one was quite sure if it answered to the head of the British or the Portuguese army – something that suited Sir Robert Wilson's independent ways of doing things.

For his part, Gen Wellesley was as anxious to get to the French as Cradock had been cautious. By 2 May, he was at Coimbra at the head of 30,000 British troops as well as 16,000 Portuguese under Marshal Beresford. On 12 May, the Anglo-Portuguese army attacked and liberated Porto. Part of Marshal Soult's army, some 9,000 men under Gen Loison, had been fighting a fierce contest for many days in late April against Gen Silveira's levies at Amarante, east of Porto, until they finally overcame the town. But this meant that, when

Maj-Gen John Francis Cradock, *c.* 1808. A veteran of the Irish 1798 campaign (where he was badly wounded) and the 1801 Egyptian campaign, he then served as Commander-in-Chief in Madras (India) before being the commanding general in Portugal. Following his replacement by Maj-Gen Wellesley in April 1809, he went on to become governor of Gibraltar and Cape Colony. (Portrait by Sir Thomas Lawrence. A print of the bust of this portrait was published on 2 January 1809. Collection of Count Vitetti, Rome. Author's photo)

Gen Wellesley attacked, Marshal Soult was outnumbered at Porto while Gen Silveira's levies, lurking around Amarante, were by no means destroyed; the writing was on the wall and the French marshal understood that retreat was the only option left. Gen Loison evacuated Amarante on 12 May and both Soult and Loison headed north through the mountains towards Spain in a harrowing winter retreat, plagued by Portuguese partisans laying ambushes, and losing much of their artillery and stores on the way. With northern Portugal secured Gen Wellesley did not pursue further and turned south 'to cooperate with the Spanish General Cuesta against the Army of Victor' (WO 1/238).

Maj-Gen Sir Arthur Wellesley takes Porto from the French on 12 May 1809. This print shows him on the heights at the monastery of Serra on the south side of the Douro River, which explains the presence of monks amongst the staff officers. (Private collection. Author's photo)

Gen Wellesley had previously sent Maj-Gen J.R. Mackenzie with 5,000 British and 7,000 Portuguese troops into eastern Portugal. This was in case, although it was improbable, that Marshal Victor might be tempted to take Alcantara and use it as a base to invade Portugal through the mountainous Tagus valley while the main British force was attacking Marshal Soult in the north; or even to go from Alcantara further north for about 30km to take the very difficult mountain pass west of Zerze la Mayor that led to Castello Branco in Portugal. This last option was most improbable given the added difficulties the extra distance would create, but either way Alcantara would have to be secured again. Since the town was as vulnerable for the British and Portuguese as it was for the French, Maj-Gen Mackenzie's army had disposed his force in the area of Castello Branco in Portugal. The Loyal Lusitanian Legion, currently under the command of Lt-Col Mayne, regrouped in eastern Portugal and was now attached to Maj-Gen Mackenzie's army. Should Marshal Victor make a move towards central Portugal, Maj-Gen Mackenzie's troops were to hold him on the upper Tagus.

With only 11,000 men, including three regiments of militia only just called up to active duty, Maj-Gen Mackenzie would have had quite a challenge containing a fully-fledged attack by the French 1st Corps. But the British and Portuguese supreme command was considering an advance – by creating a diversion while Wellesley moved on Soult's French at Porto. At that point, Victor's communications with Soult's 2nd and Ney's 6th corps in the north were completely cut off thanks to the Spanish guerrilla bands that controlled the roads and the passes in upper Estremadura and Leon. The actions of the Loyal Lusitanian Legion had certainly encouraged them enormously and, perhaps as importantly, had showed them how a small force of light troops, mounted or on foot, could control almost everything outside of city walls. Marshal Victor had his challenges too, because recent intelligence information pointed to much activity in Gen Cuesta's Spanish army, and that could only mean that his southern flank might be threatened. In a way, the timing for a diversion was ideal.

The change of command had produced amazing results. From a defeatist mindset, the British force in Portugal had instantly become more aggressive from the day Gen Wellesley arrived. Other changes of command, much lower down the organisation, were also made. For the Loyal Lusitanian Legion, Sir Robert Wilson was called to serve with Gen Wellesley's staff, no doubt because of his familiarity with the northern part of Portugal. Command of the legion had thus devolved to Lt-Col Mayne. On 27 April, Benjamin D'Urban, Quartermaster General of the Portuguese army advised Lt-Col Mayne that Marshal Beresford, no doubt in accordance with Gen Wellesley, instructed that he was 'to proceed immediately, with the Loyal Lusitanian Legion under your command, to Alcantara'. He was also to bring 'the guns and howitzers attached to the Legion'.

Lt-Col Grant would also join him, and the mustered Idanha Militia Regiment was expected to reach Castello Branco on 3 May; it would join Grant's force a few days later. The objective was laid out as follows: '...on your arrival at Alcantara, you will make such a disposition of your force as

A mountain road in Spain or Portugal, early 19th century. In general, mules and donkeys were the best means of transport in the mountain ranges of both countries and were widely used by armies criss-crossing the Iberian Peninsula. This was likely how the Loyal Lusitanian Legion moved its supplies and mountain guns through the mountains. (Period print after Foulquier. Private collection. Author's photo)

shall appear to you best for the defence of the passage of the Tagus at that place. This is an object of great importance and you will therefore take every measure necessary to ensure it.'

The 1st Battalion of the Loyal Lusitanian Legion was fit for service and, with the artillery, would be the backbone of the force. A company of the 11th Portuguese Cavalry was attached to Lt-Col Mayne and his legionnaires and they departed for Alcantara, which was reached at the beginning of May. The town itself could not be defended against a strong force, but the invaders would have to cross the Roman bridge to go on to Portugal. Situated just outside the town, it spanned very steep cliffs on both sides of the river, making it the only possible crossing in the area for any sort of commercial transport or large military force. The Romans had built it in the right place and it was a superb structure. After some 1,700 years the bridge was still very sturdy. The one place where a stand might be made was at the far side of the bridge and the legionnaires dug trenches and laid their few guns to cover the bridge's span and its immediate surroundings.

Napoleon in his imperial coronation robes, 1804. (Painting on porcelain after Jacques-Louis David. Porcelain Museum, Florence, Italy. Author's photo)

The legion's artillery company was provided with four brass 4-pdr cannons and two brass 5½in light howitzers 'with tumbrels and harness complete' and perhaps even 'some Shrapnell spherical shot', all of which had been shipped from England to Portugal. The light howitzers appear to have been British, but the 4-pdr light guns were reported as French. This was not a calibre used by the British Board of Ordnance so these guns must have been captured weapons that were issued to the Legion. They would have most likely been Gribeauval-pattern guns that had been introduced into the French artillery in 1764, and very good light pieces they were. The Portuguese were also familiar with light artillery. Since 1764, they had developed light pieces for mountain artillery. These were 3-pdrs, were moved by mules and complete with collapsible carriages. It appears that 4-pdrs, a calibre also used by the Portuguese since they had adopted the Gribeauval system in the 1790s, could also be used in this context as the pieces were light enough. In 1809, the Portuguese army was being reorganized and its artillerymen sought all the light pieces they could acquire to reorganize mountain artillery detachments. Portugal was not renowned for its good highways. When it came to the mountains, to find a decent road was a challenge indeed and much of the country's freight was carried on the back of sure-footed mules, moving on the narrow trail-like roads that crisscrossed the steep hills and mountains.

It seems that mountain carriages were used for these guns. There is no certainty that this was the case, but that type of carriage was ideally suited for the purpose. It could be carried by mules in rough terrain and quickly assembled for action, which did not exclude its being used as an ordinary 'travelling' carriage when better roads were at hand. Considering the hill terrain in the Alcantara area as well as the speed at which these guns seem to have been moved, this seems likely. That mules carried them appears most likely as Gen Wellesley, as well as Moore and Cradock before him, complained of the lack of animals (including mules) to transport artillery, and even requested that some should be sent from England.

Lt-Col Mayne's force numbered about 2,000 men, part of which was composed of militiamen. Exact returns do not appear to exist, but, on 18 April, Marshal Beresford mentioned that each of its two battalions, numbering '1,000 Rank & File each' when reporting to Lord Castlereagh, had 'behaved in the most conspicuously & gallant manner & deserve the greatest applause' and that 'the conduct of this corps plainly shows that the people of Portugal are capable of being made excellent soldiers' (WO 1/239). The last part of his remarks addressed a widespread opinion in 1809 England that, while the Portuguese and Spanish would fight, the fact that they kept losing against Napoleon's troops meant that they were poor and ill-trained soldiers on the battlefield. While this largely remained the case with regard to Spanish troops, the Portuguese army was evolving and would become, especially its infantry, one of Europe's most lethal forces in terms of steadiness and firepower; equal to the fearsome British line, according to its French opponents. In a sense, as events were to show, the Loyal Lusitanian Legion was something of a forerunner in this transformation of the Portuguese army. But, in the spring of 1809, this process was just beginning. As to the actual strength of the 1st Battalion that went to Alcantara, Mayne and Lillie's account suggests that it was some 750 men, although a report of the battle in the 1809 *Correio braziliense* mentions only 600, which seems low. The detachment of the 11th Portuguese Cavalry numbered about 50 troopers; the troop was probably indifferently mounted seeing that there were widespread shortages of horses in Portugal, but they were certainly useful as scouts. According to Mayne, the Idanha Militia Regiment numbered 1,200 men that had been recently called to active duty. The Portuguese militia itself was in the midst of a full reorganization, like the regular army, and it may be surmised that the officers and men of this unit, while considered fit enough for service and probably better trained and appointed than most other militia regiments, were nevertheless the weakest part of the force sent to Alcantara.

Besides creating defences at Alcantara, some of Mayne's men under Lt-Col Grant went further east and southeast, roaming around the countryside looking for the French. They soon found detachments scouting, just as they were. The French were no doubt surprised to encounter what were obviously regular British or Portuguese skirmishers now operating between Alcantara

11 MAY 1809

Marshal Victor begins march towards Alcantara

and Merida. It was soon noted that they had occupied Alcantara. The news was relayed to Marshal Victor who was duly worried. Most likely advised by Gen Lapisse, who had been grappling with these green-coated troops in Leon, there was no doubt that these were no ordinary peasant levies or guerrillas. It could be the vanguard of an Anglo-Portuguese force wishing to penetrate Estremadura. Should such a move succeed, his 1st Corps would then have to face this new enemy while facing the threat of Gen Cuesta's Spanish army joining in on his southern flank. On the other hand, it might be just a small forward force using Alcantara as an outpost and that it would go no further – which it indeed was.

Another grave factor that Victor had to consider (as did any French marshal) was Napoleon's imperial will. Victor's 1st Corps had not stirred at all while Soult was invading northern Portugal, with Marshal Ney's small 6th Corps trying to hold Galicia in support. But that was all Victor knew. Communications with Galicia being cut off by the guerrillas, no one had current news on how Marshal Soult was doing in Portugal. The most recent word reaching King Joseph's headquarters in Madrid had been from 22 April, when it was reported that Soult had taken Porto. Good news, but that event had occurred a full month before King Joseph heard about it. No doubt he had sent a courier to advise Marshal Victor. But even assuming the marshal received such a message by early May, he was totally ignorant of what had occurred to Soult since, and nor did he have any idea of his enemy's strength within Portugal.

One thing was certain, and that was Napoleon's wrath if he concluded that Marshal Victor had just sat inactive in Merida, contrary to imperial orders. Indeed, what would the emperor say when he learned that the strategically important Alcantara had not even been left with a French garrison? And with Napoleon's humours came either rewards or withdrawal of favours and consideration. Still another factor was that, if Soult was successful and in fact progressing in Portugal, he would get all the glory and riches while Victor would have nothing but censure for having stayed in Estremadura. So, the better option was to advance upon Alcantara, take the place and go into eastern Portugal to create a diversion. Whatever was happening to Marshal Soult's force, it was a good political move for Marshal Victor. He still had to worry about the Spanish army on his southern flank, so the whole 1st Corps could not be devoted to the advance on Alcantara. Marshal Victor chose Gen Lapisse's 2nd Division, no doubt because it was already familiar with Alcantara, as regrettably seen above, and with that peculiar and most troublesome corps of Anglo-Portuguese skirmishers. Part of Latour-Maubourg's dragoons were attached since the French force had 1,500 cavalry (which included the 5th and 12th Dragoons) and the train of artillery taken along consisted of a dozen 8- and 12-pdr field guns. In all, with various other detachments, the force was estimated at 10,000 to 12,000 men led by Marshal Victor himself.

ALCANTARA BRIDGE

Thus Victor led his force out of Merida on 11 May and on to the road to Alcantara. This time the chips were down and there was a big difference with the past actions of the Loyal Lusitanian Legion: although a corps of raiders and skirmishers, it now had to make a stand. As usual, the enemy was much stronger, but this was the usual situation in the field for men like Mayne, Grant and all the legionnaires. As events eventually unfolded however, the part of Mayne's command made up of militiamen worried a great deal more about being grossly outnumbered at odds of six to one.

Whatever the odds, Marshal Victor did not have to wait until he got to Alcantara to meet up with a a Loyal Lusitanian Legion detachment led by Lt-Col Grant who naturally 'retired before the enemy's corps' while keeping an eye on its movement and pace. As the French got near to Alcantara early on 14 May, there was 'some skirmishing' between them and Grant's men at about 8am. Marshal Victor had disposed them in three columns as they neared Alcantara and Lt-Col Grant had 'ascertained their strength, 10,000 infantry, 1500 cavalry, and 12 pieces of artillery, some of them 8 and other 12-pounders'. There was thus no point in putting up a fight in the town, which must have been empty of any inhabitants by then. Some of the legion's guns were there to greet them since Mayne later related that 'our artillery fired with great effect on the enemy entering the town, covering at the same time Lieutenant-Colonel Grant as he passed with his detachment over the bridge to join me'. Thus Grant's men retreated through Alcantara and, running down towards the bridge and crossing it, taking the light guns with them, probably exchanged a few shots with French voltigeurs or cavalrymen in the process, before taking their positions with the rest of the defenders. They were likely disposed in the various lines of trenches built across the way: 'the infantry … formed on the heights, under the cover of some temporary breast works.' The Loyal Lusitanian Legion men would have been in the first line with the Idanha militiamen in support behind. The rocky cliff running down from the road to the river likely offered some of the better shots the legion could take and if there were a few riflemen,

Private of the Idanha Militia Regiment, c. 1809. According to the 1806 regulations, Portuguese militia regiments had dark blue coatees faced with various distinctive colours at the collar and cuffs, with piping and turnbacks of the division's hue. For Idanha, this consisted of dark blue cuffs with red collar, piping and turnbacks. Militiamen were also to wear a round hat with a fur crest going over its crown and a yellow plume rising on the left side from Portugal's national red and blue cockade. This figure is, of course, an ideal representation of this uniform; the reality was most probably more in tune with the supply difficulties experienced in Portugal at the time; the round hats, for instance, might not have the crest or plume. The arms and accoutrements supplied to the Portuguese militia units were from Britain, some of them previously used by British militia corps. (Plate by William Younghusband, © Osprey Publishing)

they would have been there to pick off whatever came into range. The disposition of the legion's six guns is unknown but they seem to have been divided into two or three groups that Mayne and Lillie rather generously called 'batteries' in spite of being most likely pairs of guns – possibly a pair on each side of the bridge and two covering its span.

Eventually, Marshal Victor and much of his corps came within sight of the Roman bridge. They now saw it blocked at its far end with lines of trenches and a few small guns with hundreds of troops in green and in blue uniforms posted on the opposite side of the river. An advance was made towards the bridge so as to impress the defenders of this position. It was a tactic that sometimes worked on raw militiamen who might panic on seeing well-appointed French regulars marching towards them. But not this time. Lt-Col Mayne, who 'was determined to dispute the passage of the river as much as possible, in conformity to the orders he had received' ordered his guns to open fire and everyone stayed put. Marshal Victor looked at the surroundings and soon realized, surely as Gen Lapisse would have told him, that there was no way to outflank the enemy position in such steep topography. And this being the spring, the fast-flowing river was high, so there was no place to ford in the area. The only solution was to take the Roman bridge by storming it.

The French therefore formed their assault columns; these would have been made up of the grenadier companies of the 8th, 45th and 54th Line regiments in front with some of the fusilier companies following them. Others would secure positions in various places on the front while light infantry voltigeurs and chasseurs lined the banks as skirmishers. The artillerymen were bringing their guns while looking for suitable places to position them, which was not easy in such a terrain. The cavalry could not deploy and looked on from a distance. As Mayne and Lillie, whose account is the only one giving some details of the fight, related, 'the parapets of the town' in the distance 'were soon lined by the infantry of the enemy, while they constructed batteries' as the assault columns moved towards the Roman bridge.

'About nine o'clock a very tremendous fire commenced from the two sides of the Tagus' and what happened next, and for hours to come, was that when the 'enemy's columns having come within range of our batteries, our guns commenced a fire on them with a good deal of effect, and many shells were pitched directly into the centre of their columns, which did considerable execution'. That four light-calibre guns and two light howitzers were able to achieve this result means that they were very well served by their gunners; the use of shells was most appropriate and there is even a possibility that they could have been the newly invented and lethal 'Shrapnell spherical shot' shells that were starting to be used in the British artillery.

14 MAY 1809

Battle of Alcantara Bridge

Trooper of the 11th Portuguese Cavalry, 1806 uniform. The regiment's dress was dark blue with sky blue collar and cuffs, red piping and turnbacks, gold buttons. The crested leather helmet was later replaced by the British-style light dragoon shako. (From a 1909 print after Ribeiro Arthur. Private collection. Author's photo)

Thus, the French columns faced a withering fire, no doubt suffering heavy casualties as they charged onto the bridge, and, by the time they would have reached the middle of the bridge, their ranks were much thinned to the point where even if they reached the defenders, there would not be enough men left to be able to carry the position. So, in all probability, the attacks would stop at about midway and what was left of the attackers obviously retreated.

It must be recalled that the Roman bridge was (and remains) a narrow causeway with thick stone walls on both sides that, in this instance, turned it into something of a shooting gallery for its the defenders. At their end of the bridge, they were certainly well positioned with their small guns protected by field fortifications featuring 'fascines, gabions, &c.' for cover that had been constructed during the previous days.

Of course, as in all battles, if one attack failed, the next one might succeed and so more assaults were attempted. And they kept being repulsed. It was time for Marshal Victor to bring up his artillery since the 'heavy and destructive fire of musketry had commenced on both sides' and this would obviously not be enough to push the defenders out of the way. Indeed, they looked like they were going to put up a stiff fight and Victor may have thought that he should have brought more artillery. As it was, he could see that he presently had more guns and that they were of heavier calibres than those of his opponents. It might take a long time, but superior firepower would come to prevail. Eventually, the morning wore on and 'the enemy having brought all their artillery to bear on us, together with the concentrated fire of eleven thousand muskets, with which the houses, &c., on the opposite side were lined' reported Mayne, it could be said that the defenders were really coming under tremendous pressure. For every shot of Mayne's men, Victor's men could fire five. But, the rate of casualties must have been relatively light for the Portuguese because they obviously delivered a fearsome fire, and the French still could not get across the bridge.

At about noon, amidst all the shooting 'which continued incessant', the militiamen of the Idanha Regiment 'not being accustomed to any thing of this kind, and witnessing their officers and men falling and wounded on every side' became totally distressed – thinking their last day on earth had come – panicked and 'made a precipitate retreat in a body' reported Lt-Col Mayne. In spite of the considerable amount of smoke that must have obscured vision in the valley, the French probably saw the hundreds of blue-coated troops running away from their position, and this would have been a great encouragement. The departure from the trenches of some 1,200 of his men, albeit the weaker ones that were not really soldiers, was certainly a heavy blow to Lt-Col Mayne. By then, between noon and one in the afternoon, the French had managed to put in battery 'seven guns all posted, bearing upon our position', which could not stand indefinitely. He now only had 'the remnant of the Loyal Lusitanian Legion, (500 men) and the batteries of artillery' that could be devoted to holding the bridge and 'occupying the heights of Alcantara'. Their heavy guns were now steadily firing at the defenders and assault columns would renew their attempts to carry the bridge at bayonet-point. For Lt-Col Mayne, who was then at his 'main battery' near or at the bridge, it was clear that the end was in sight. But he still had a card up his sleeve: blow up the bridge!

Amongst the preparations previously made to defend the position, Lt-Col Mayne had his men – probably the gunners – install a mine under one of the spans of the bridge. The time had come to consider this option. Half of the defenders had panicked and 'basely left' the position, putting the odds at 20-to-one in favour of the French. True, the Idanha Militia was hardly a seasoned fighting force, but its departure turned the defence from being very difficult to impossible. The seasoned raiders of the Loyal Lusitanian Legion were turning into very obstinate and redoubtable defenders, but this could not last – if only because ammunition was starting to run low; the intense shooting had been going on for over four hours. The time had therefore come and, at about 1pm or thereafter, Lt-Col Mayne 'thought it advisable to put fire to the mine of the bridge of Alcantara'. It was accordingly done and the explosion must have caused a tremendous tremor with fire, falling debris and smoke covering the area. Once the smoke cleared, the French must have been somewhat relieved while the defenders surely gasped in disbelief. The explosion 'only blew up on one side [of the bridge], leaving a free passage for the enemy across the Tagus.'

Once he had appreciated the remarkable resilience of Roman engineering, Lt-Col Mayne felt he 'had only one resort [left], which was, to give Lieutenant-Colonel Grant the command of the main battery, as the only means of preventing the enemy immediately pressing upon me while I effected a retreat'. Grant would stay with a rearguard and one gun at the bridge to fire on anything that ventured onto the remaining span of the bridge, while the rest of the force would withdraw with the other five pieces of artillery. As for the few troopers of the 11th Cavalry, they had been 'reduced by fatigue from 50 to 20, [and] were no[t able to] cover me'. So covering the retreat was left to the detachment with the gun at the bridge. It was agreed to 'sacrifice one field-piece for the security of the three others and the two howitzers'.

How long this resistance went on is somewhat unclear. Lt-Col Mayne related that 'Lieutenant-Colonel Grant [was] very ready to undertake the fighting of the main battery with this one piece [of artillery at the bridge]. I moved away with the other five [guns], and he did this [fighting] from two o'clock to three... Our ammunition being nearly wasted, and our killed and wounded surrounding us, it was absolutely necessary to adopt this mode of retreat with the few brave Lusitanians that were left; and to secure my artillery, the remaining gun was spiked and rendered of no use to the enemy on Lieutenant-Colonel Grant's leaving it to its fate after he had continued to fire it for one hour to the great deception of the enemy, giving me time enough to pass the plain country...'

Just when the retreat took place is also somewhat unclear. Lt-Col Mayne's report to Maj-Gen Mackenzie is quoted above, but when he summed up the situation in his narrative with Capt Lillie, he stated:

'...but much to the credit of the brave soldiers engaged, be it recorded, that they sustained that tremendous fire for the space of nine hours, during

THE BATTLE OF ALCANTARA BRIDGE

ABOUT 1pm, 14 MAY 1809

The most spectacular event in the remarkable defence of Alcantara bridge, conducted by a small Portuguese force under Lt-Col Mayne and against Marshal Victor's hordes of French troops, was certainly the explosion of part of its span. The battle had been fiercely fought since nine in the morning; by noon, the men of the Idanha Militia in Mayne's force 'not being accustomed to any thing of this kind' broke and fled leaving only the few hundred regular legionnaires to defend the bridge. Although they were managing to repulse the French with their small cannons and their muskets, this could not last forever and ammunition would run

low. Explosives had been installed under a bridge span and Lt-Col Mayne now 'thought it advisable to put fire to the mine of the bridge of Alcantara.' It was fired and this is the moment shown on our bird's-eye view illustration. The whole area would have been covered by much smoke from the constant firing of the seven French guns, the six Portuguese ones and many thousands of muskets.

KEY

1	French infantry
2	French artillery (probable positions)
3	Marshal Victor's HQ/Command post (probable position)
4	Bridge blows up
5	Loyal Lusitanian Legion infantry (probable positions)
6	Loyal Lusitanian Legion artillery (probable positions)
7	Lt-Col Mayne's command post (probable position)

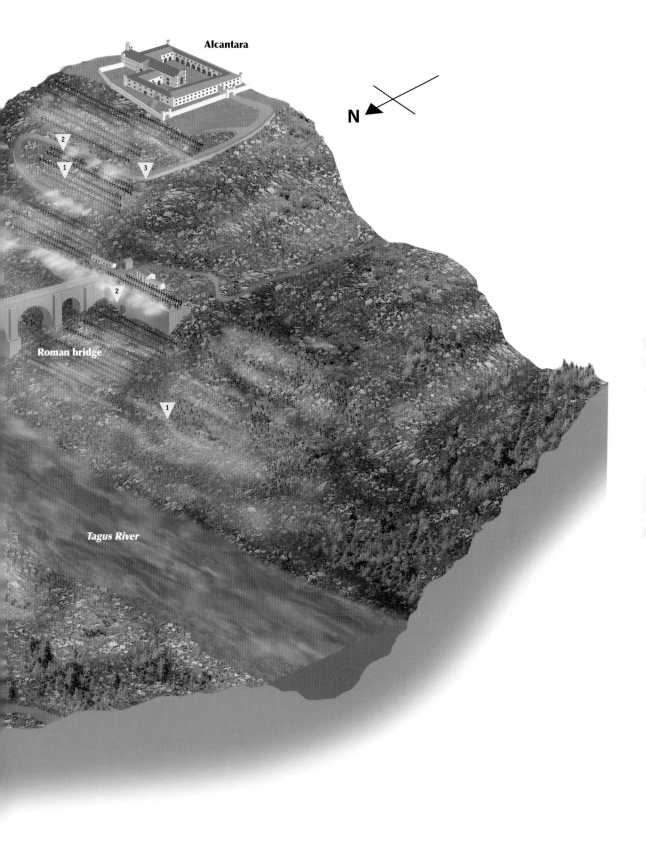

Alcantara

Roman bridge

Tagus River

N

which the enemy could not succeed in any attempt made at carrying the bridge by storm, having suffered most considerably from the well directed fire of our sharpshooters, covered by the rocks, &c., within forty or fifty yards of the bridge, and from that to one and two hundred yards along the ascent of the heights. However, night coming on, which would evidently favour them, and especially in any attempt at carrying the bridge by storm, in which by the vast superiority of their numbers they must ultimately succeed, together with our small force already reduced by the loss of seven officers and two hundred and fifty men killed and wounded, Colonel Mayne was induced, to prevent the complete sacrifice of these brave fellows under his command, to retire to the bridge of Seguro, only two leagues distant, leaving a rear guard with the cavalry, under Lieutenant Colonel Grant, to cover this movement, which was effected with the greatest steadiness and regularity…'

According to this text, the defence of Alcantara bridge had gone on for nine hours, starting at nine in the morning and therefore ending at six in the early evening. In his report, the last shots with the remaining 4-pdr were fired at about three in the afternoon, after which it was spiked. Thus, it seems that the rearguard under Lt-Col Grant reverted to its skirmishing raiders' tactics and kept shooting at the French from covered positions as they were retreating.

When and how the French finally did cross the bridge is also murky, but at last they made it to the other side of the river Tagus. A French cavalry detachment of about 100 men soon caught up with some of the retreating

Marshal Victor, c. 1826. Claude-Victor Perrin was known as Victor. He became marshal in 1807 and duke of Bellune the following year. (Unsigned portrait. Musée de l'Armée, Paris. Author's photo)

force, when Lt-Col Grant's men were joining the main force. The French cavalry, Lt-Col Mayne reported to Maj-Gen Mackenzie, 'appeared on the Alcantara side of the bridge at Seguro' where the legionnaires were to move into new defence positions. But the French troopers 'were close to us, and ready to move upon my infantry, who were much exposed…' As it turned out, the French cavalrymen were somewhat nervous too while the Portuguese quickly resorted to a ruse de guerre, fooling them into thinking they were about to be attacked. This was done by letting four horsemen, almost certainly troopers of the 11th Portuguese Cavalry, face them at front while some skirmishers opened 'a distant firing' from covered positions. Lt-Col Mayne expected more action, but the French cavalrymen 'unexpectedly retired' – all the way back to Alcantara, it was later learned.

Thus ended the battle for Alcantara bridge. By midnight, Lt-Col Mayne made his report, which included a count of his casualties. The Loyal Lusitanian Legion had four officers (all Portuguese) and 103 rank and file killed, four officers (including Lt-Col Grant slightly and Lt Mendoza who later died) and 143 rank and file wounded, and two subalterns and 15 rank and file missing. The casualties of the Idanha Militia Regiment show that they endured quite a lot before they broke and ran. Its 'butcher's bill' came to three officers and 40 rank and file killed, one officer and 17 rank and file wounded, two subaltern officers and 1,150 missing. This last entry is interesting as it reveals its officers did not panic, but instead must have tried to restrain their men and ultimately remained with the legionnaires. This probably explains why the unit was not censured by Marshal Beresford later on.

As is often the case with the French army in the smaller engagements of the Peninsular War, its casualties at Alcantara are unknown. The only casualty found was that of 5th Dragoons Lt Massier's horse pierced by four bayonet wounds, seemingly early in the engagement. Whatever they were, they do not seem to have been slight – if we are to believe Mayne and Lillie's account of the day's fighting that went on there. A later British report estimated that the French force's loss 'at least amounted to 1,400 men'. Perhaps somewhat high, but this author feels that it may not be that far-fetched. As it is, it is the only figure we have so far from a contemporary document, the legion's narrative printed in 1812.

The subsequent days demonstrated that Marshal Victor was quite cautious and did not go much further although Maj-Gen Mackenzie at Castello Branco was far from sure as to what to expect. Lt-Col Mayne's troops therefore were to continue keeping a watch on the movements of the French in the upper Tagus valley. The legionnaires were now in a new defensive position at the bridge at Seguro, which was a far less scenic one than the Roman bridge, but nevertheless meant another river crossing under fire for the French. Some of Marshal Victor's troops advanced towards this position, 'which they reconnoitred, sustaining at the same time some loss from our skirmishers', thus showing that the green-clad raiders were back to their old ways. At about this time, Marshal Victor obtained information to the effect that Marshal Soult had been beaten and chased out of northern Portugal. This meant Napoleon's invasion of Portugal was off, which was

OVERLEAF: The defence of the Roman bridge at Alcantara, 14 May 1809

While the officers and men of the Loyal Lusitanian Legion were superlative raiders, they could transform themselves into a most stubborn defence force if they had a good position. Thus it was that, for some nine hours, part of the 2nd French Army Corps led by Marshal Victor could not cross the bridge defended by the legionnaires in spite of repeated assaults, artillery bombardments and gruelling musketry by over 10,000 troops. The plate shows two light guns of the legion posted on the bridge to cover its span. They probably opened up a murderous anti-personnel fire when a French assault would be about to reach the arch in the middle. The defence force, eventually reduced to a few hundred legionnaires, expertly used its six small guns and muskets. In spite of odds of twenty to one, this extraordinary band of green-coated soldiers – worthy of the best modern commandos – made an orderly retreat saving five of their guns in the process and, the next day, were ready to contest the passage of the Tagus River at another crossing about 10km away. Three days later, Marshal Victor evacuated Alcantara and went back east.

A Recollection of the bridge of Alcantara
June 1810 –

'A Recollection of the bridge of Alcantara, June 1810' by Alexander Dickson. This recollection was probably drawn years later since it shows a few doubtful items – the foremost being that it was the fifth and not the sixth arch that was blown up. The presence of large turrets and fairly extensive medieval-looking walls is also questionable and not supported by other sources. The turret on the north side still exists today and it is a smaller structure. The south side still has its small Roman temple not visible here. The medieval fortifications were said to be mostly in ruins and houses were mentioned to be near the Roman temple. (Author's photo)

surely a relief, because news was arriving from Merida relating that Gen Cuesta's army was moving north.

On 17 May, the French army evacuated Alcantara and went back to Merida. According to Mayne and Lillie, an intercepted letter signed by Marshal Victor stated that 'in the course of his service he never witnessed more intrepidity than was evinced by these young Portuguese soldiers at the battle of Alcantara'. Ten days later, Marshal Beresford approved, in a General Order to the Portuguese army, 'this brave conduct, and bestows upon them his greatest praises. He cannot avoid observing at the same time that both battalions of the Loyal Lusitanian Legion have always distinguished themselves, on all occasions, which have been many' (WO 1/1121).

Meanwhile, Lt-Col Mayne and his legionnaires, now reinforced by the Portuguese 5th Battalion of Caçadores (light infantry) and a battalion of the Covilhas Militia, had stayed in the vicinity of Alcantara watching what movements Marshal Victor would make. Having ascertained that the French, and especially Lapisse's division, were not likely to be back, Gen Mackenzie instructed Lt-Col Mayne and his force to again occupy Alcantara, which was done seemingly in late May. In time, the inhabitants also trickled back into their devastated town, and one of these was the Prior of the Knightly Military Order of Alcantara. When he saw Lt-Col Mayne, an emotional and symbolic event took place: the Prior went up to him and, 'insisting on taking the Cross of the Order from his own breast', affixed it to Lt-Col Mayne. He must have been the first Englishman to receive the honour of being made a knight of the Order of Alcantara.

ANALYSIS

For the Loyal Lusitanian Legion, a five-month period of raids as well as a most notable battle came to an end in mid-May 1809. At that time, raid warfare and covert operations were then in their infancy as tactical options. Sir Robert Wilson's daring was certainly a sizeable gamble, but it was well calculated. He was an experienced leader and a man who took risks. He loved the freedom that independent action in remote areas brought and was aware that success in what we now call raid warfare could only be possible with a regular unit of physically sturdy, well trained and steady men of proven bravery who would be able to deploy speedily, much faster than ordinary troops. In effect, the part of the legion that was under his personal command on the plains of Leon became akin to a modern commando unit. His officers, notably lieutenants-colonels Mayne and Grant, were well versed and obviously enthusiastic in the tactical practice of raid warfare.

The primary objective of Wilson and his men was to keep as many enemy troops as possible on alert. In this, they succeeded admirably during the whole period. A small battalion with a few light pieces kept an army division with additional cavalry on its toes and in confusion for months. There was also much activity from the Spanish irregulars and regulars, but these were usually easily swept aside by the French – with the exception of Don Julian Sanchez's guerrillas. Thus, the French's main permanent contender on the plains of Leon was usually the Lusitanian corps of light troops. That their opponents had some British officers and were seemingly Portuguese was also the source of some wild speculation as to who and what they really were: a large British and Portuguese force? A division of up to 12,000 enemies? No one really knew and with communications cut off by the guerrillas, even news from the other French armies was very scant, let alone trusty intelligence about the British and Portuguese.

When the French division finally managed to march south and sack Alcantara to join Marshal Victor, hit-and-run tactics were no longer the prime means of keeping the French in a defensive position in terms of overall strategy. Marshal Victor's corps was supposed to assist in the invasion of

The Roman bridge at Altancara, about mid-1809. The span of the second arch from the north bank of the Tagus River was totally destroyed after 14 May 1809. There has been some confusion as to which arch went up, because of Dickson's statement that it was the first arch, but a sketch by Maj Sturgeon, who built a temporary wooden and rope suspension span on it in 1812, plus Hay's account and this contemporary print leave no doubt that Dickson made an understandable error and that it was in fact the second arch. (Private collection. Author's photo)

Portugal, but kept to watching the large Spanish army in Andalucia. When the news came that the strategically important town of Alcantara had been occupied by those rather mysterious Portuguese troops led by British officers, the place simply had to be retaken. The outstanding defence at the bridge by Lt-Col Mayne's men was a classic example, probably one of the first ones, of what a commando-style light corps holding a favourable position could do against masses of enemy assaults and heavy bombardment. The legion's good use of light ordnance as an anti-personnel weapon was also proven to be most valuable for light troops in such instances. And, finally, damaging the Roman bridge meant rendering crossings quite difficult in an immediate invasion scenario.

Of course, skirmishing went on as well during this later phase. As far as one can tell, it continued to be nearly always to the advantage of the legionnaires. The French had light troops too, so why were they unable to stem the legion's raids? Their 2nd Division had three battalions of the '16e Léger' (16th Light Infantry) that, in February 1809, would have mustered about 1,800 to 2,000 officers and men, about double Sir Robert Wilson's force. They were indeed supposed to move faster, but more as fast-paced battalions, fanning in front of their line infantry. The same could be said of French light cavalry, although none appears to have been consistently deployed in this area; dragoons were fearsome too, but were slower. Thus, the French light troops do not seem to have come up with or applied a tactical doctrine that could deal efficiently with commando-type raiders.

CONCLUSION

Alcantara had been once again secured by the Portuguese troops. Marshal Victor now knew that, instead of invading the enemy, he would likely soon be facing British as well as Portuguese and Spanish troops. While he was away at Alcantara, Gen Cuesta's army had prodded his defences at Merida. The countryside was nearly barren of supplies and many inhabitants had abandoned their villages. The result was that the French troops were now on half-rations and thousands were in bad health. Reinforcements were almost useless unless they came with plenty of supplies, and this was unlikely as French armies usually lived off the country they were in. The marshal therefore appraised King Joseph that a retreat from Estremadura was advisable.

The battle of Talavera. Fought in Spanish territory, 120km south-west of Madrid, Wellesley's victory resulted in his ennoblement as Viscount Wellington of Talavera. (Anne S.K. Brown Military Collection, Brown University Library, Providence, USA)

The Roman bridge repaired, 1830s. It is said that it was repaired in 1860, but this anonymous print published in 1837 shows that some repairs were made before that – unless the artist copied an unknown work predating 1809. An illustration of the bridge in *The Penny Magazine* of 29 August 1835 also shows the bridge with all its masonry spans. (Private collection. Author's photo)

King Joseph promised supplies for the 1st Corps and beckoned that it should retake and hold Alcantara instead. Marshal Victor replied that this would be just about useless as he had learned that, on 8 June, the remaining part of the bridge span that had not been destroyed in the explosion during the battle had been blown up. Lt-Col Mayne wanted to make sure it would be next to useless for the French. He and his Portuguese troops were later much criticised by the Spanish for this action. Dickson related that they were 'very angry at its having been broke, and more so, as it has since been ascertained that it was done in consequence of the approach of a small body of cavalry only. They say that the bridge was permitted by the Goths, Moors, and other barbarous nations to exist without injury, but that at last it was destroyed by the Portuguese who are the most barbarous of all.' As can be seen, the old grudges between the Spanish and the Portuguese were never far from the surface. Even in our times, French journalist Michel Deom felt they seemed to share the same peninsula back to back rather than deign to look at each other…

In military terms however, blowing up the span may have in fact averted another attempt on Alcantara had Marshal Victor followed up on King Joseph's wish. On 10 June, King Joseph finally learned, via Paris, that Marshal Soult had indeed been routed by Gen Wellesley and that his British army would likely be marching southeast. It was time to regroup the forces and Marshal Victor was allowed to evacuate, which he did from 14 June; the bridges over the Guadiana River at Medellin and Merida were blown up by the retreating 1st Corps that posted itself in the area of Talavera de la Reina.

There, at Talavera, would be written the next chapter of the Peninsular War.

FURTHER READING AND SELECT BIBLIOGRAPHY

The raids in western Spain and at Alcantara did not result in a stream of publications or even of detailed reports of documents in the archives. Indeed, this appears to be the first book that examines this relatively unknown period of the Peninsular War. The main British histories of the Peninsular War and of the British army by Sir Charles Oman and Sir John Fortescue do mention it in passing, as does Portuguese historian Simao José da Luz Soriano's 'Historia da Guerra…' and all are based on Mayne and Lillie's 'A Narrative of Campaigns…' No other English or Portuguese detailed memoirs appear to have been published on these events. As for French sources, they are sparse and misleading, although one cannot be too surprised at this considering their performance in what was to them a far-off sideshow in an unpopular war. Even Martinien's compilation of officer casualties are silent on actions in Leon and at Alcantara while Hugo's summary of the Napoleonic campaigns is equally mute – although useful in the general context. Other French sources that do mention Alcantara are cited below, but there are no in-depth accounts and the engagement is given, of course, to the glory of Marshal Victor. They have obviously ignored the one Spanish source by the Conde de Toreno, translated into French, for whom it is a success for the allies. Archives may contain detailed reports, but, if they exist, they would be in remote files not yet found by historians. The National Archives of the United Kingdom in Kew do have a number of documents on the Loyal Lusitanian Legion with passing references to its officers and the events covered in this book. These are in some volumes of the War Office series 1 and 6 and Foreign Office 63 (cited in text as WO or FO with series and volume number, i.e.: WO 1/230).

Nevertheless, when the various pieces are put together, a picture emerges: that of the fascinating raids and counter-raids in remote and half-forgotten western Spain in those desperate times when some men would not bow to the Emperor of the French.

Published works

'Alcantara', *The Penny Magazine*, 29 August 1835.

Belmas, Jacques, *Journaux des sièges faits ou soutenus par les Français dans la Péninsule*, Paris (1836), Vol. 1. Valuable for reproducing letters between the French commanders.

Bonaparte, Joseph, *Mémoires et correspondance politique et militaire du roi Joseph*, edited by Albert Du Casse, Paris (1854), Vol. 6.

Burnham, Robert, 'The destruction of the bridge at Alcantara: 14 May, 1809', *The Napoleon Series* at: http://www.napoleon-series.org/military/virtual/c_alcantara.html.

Chaby, Claudio de, *Excerptos Historicos e Collecçao de Documentos Relativos à Guerra Denominada da Peninsula...*, Vol. III, Lisbon (1865).

Chartrand, René, 'Sir Robert Wilson and the Loyal Lusitanian Legion 1808–1811', *Journal of the Society for Army Historical Research*, (2001), pp. 197–208.

Chartrand, René, *Spanish Guerrillas in the Peninsular War 1808–1814*, Osprey Elite 108: Oxford (2004).

Correio braziliense, ou, *Armazem literario*, London (1809), Volume 2. Contains at pages 630–636 a Portuguese account based on Lt-Col Mayne's dispatch of the 14 May battle and names the officers who were casualties.

Dickson, Alexander, *The Dickson Manuscripts: Being Diaries, Letters Maps, Account Books, with Various Other Papers...*, edited by J.H. Leslie, Woolwich (1908), chapter II (for the year 1810). Dickson provided a good description of the Roman bridge at Alcantara as well as other useful statistical information.

D'Urban, Benjamin, *The Peninsular Journal of Major General Sir Benjamin D'Urban 1808–1817*, edited by L.J. Rousseau, London (1930).

Fortescue, J.W., *A History of the British Army*, Macmillan & Co.: London (1935), Vol. VII.

Griffon de Pleineville, Natalia, *La Corogne*, LCV: Paris (2009). The most complete and lavishly illustrated account of the Corunna campaign and much more besides.

Halliday, Andrew, *The Present State of Portugal and of the Portuguese Army*, Edinburgh (1812).

Hay, Andrew Leith, *A Narrative of the Peninsular War*, London (1850).

History of the Campains of the British forces in Spain and Portugal..., London (1813), Vol. 4. Also reproduces documents in Mayne and Lillie's accounts.

Hugo, Abel, *France Militaire*, Paris (1837), Vol. 4.

Le Noble, Pierre, *Mémoires sur les opérations militaires des Français: en Galice, en Portugal, et dans la vallée du Tage, en 1809, sous le commandement du Maréchal Soult, Duc de Damatie*, Paris (1821).

Lignières, Marie-Henry de, *Souvenirs de la Grande Armée et de la vieille garde impériale*, Paris (1933). Lignières was detached to the area of Salamanca in 1809, did not encounter the legionnaires, but often fought Spaniards who were always routed. His account nevertheless gives a rare glimpse of the war in Leon as seen from the French side.

The elaborate green-on-white cross of the Knights of the Order of Alcantara (Wikimedia)

Luz Soriano, Simao José da, *Historia da Guerra Civil*, Lisbon (1871), Segunda epocha, Tome II. Fine Portuguese history of the Peninsular War.

Martinien, Aristide, *Tableaux par corps et par batailles des officiers tués et blessés pendant les guerres de l'Empire (1805–1815)*, Paris (1899).

Mayne, William and John Scott Lillie. *A Narrative of Campaigns of the Loyal Lusitanian Legion during the Years 1809, 1810 & 1811*, London (1812). The most important source for this study. It contains what seems to be the only somewhat detailed account of the legion's activities in Leon as well as Estremadura.

Mayne, William, *On the First Portuguese Legion, the documents of Colonel Mayne*, London (1810). This 44 page booklet is the first version of the expanded 'Narrative…' published with the assistance of Capt. Lillie in 1812, quoted above. It appears to be extremely rare, the only copy known to the author being inserted in WO 1/1121 at The National Archives of Great Britain.

Moeller, Charles, 'Military Order of Alcantara.' *The Catholic Encyclopaedia*, New York (1907), Vol. 1.

O Investigador portuguez em Inglaterra: ou, Jornal literário, London, 1818. On p. 437 mentions the repulse and rout of the French at Alcantara.

Oman, Charles, *A History of the Peninsular War*, Oxford (1903), Vol. 2. The finest British history of the war.

Quei po de Llano Ruiz de Saravia Toreno, Conde de Toreno, José-Maria, *Histoire du soulèvement, de la guerre et de la révolution d'Espagne*, Paris (1836), Vol. 3. Translated from the Spanish, partly based on Mayne and Lillie, and the better account in French of the Alcantara battles.

Rocca, Albert Jean M. de la, *Mémoires sur la guerre des Français en Espagne*, Paris (1814). Reports on page 120 that Marshal Victor crossed the Tagus River and went into Portugal following 'an engagement of little importance against Portuguese militias' at Alcantara (the bridge is not mentioned), the typical misinformation from French propaganda.

Saint-Just, V. de, *Historique du 5e Régiment de Dragons*, Paris (1891).

Sao Carlos, Friar Ignacio do, 'Jornal' in Christovam Ayres de Magalhaes Sepulveda, *Historia Organica e Politica do Exercito Portugues*, Vol., XIII, Coimbra (1923).

Selvagem, Carlos, *Portugal Militar: Compendio de Historia Militar e Naval de Portugal*, Lisbon (1931).

Smith, Digby, *Napoleonic Wars Data Book*, Greenhill: London (1998).

Thiers, Adolphe, *Histoire du Consulat et de l'Empire*, Brussels (1851), Vol. 11. Mixes the two captures of Alcantara by attributing to Marshal Victor an outstanding victory 'over the insurgents who were put through the sword'.

INDEX

Figures in **bold** refer to illustrations